THE
bread
COLLECTION

ARTISAN BAKING FOR THE BREAD ENTHUSIAST

BRIAN HART HOFFMAN

THE
bread
COLLECTION

ARTISAN BAKING FOR THE
BREAD ENTHUSIAST

83Press
1900 International Park Drive, Suite 50
Birmingham, Alabama 35243

ISBN: 978-1-940772-56-1
Printed in China

contents

Baking bread stimulates the senses
unlike any other experience in the kitchen.

FROM FORMING THE DOUGH TO INHALING ITS RICH, BUTTERY
SCENT AS IT BAKES, THE WARM COMFORT ONE RECEIVES
FROM BAKING BREAD GOES BEYOND PHYSICAL NOURISHMENT;
IT'S NOURISHMENT FOR THE SOUL.

For those both new and well-accustomed to the wonders of bread, I assembled *The Bread Collection*, my ode to all things dough.

Acting as both a brilliant reference book and exhaustive recipe collection of my all-time favorite bread recipes, this cookbook enables home bakers of all levels to take on any bread project. From Old World-style yeasted wreaths and Irish soda breads to modern takes on scones and muffins. You'll find nutty, fruity, and chocolaty twists on brioche, babka, and challah as well as simple but epic recipes for buttermilk biscuits, Dutch oven bread, and sourdough. From kneading and proofing to shaping and baking, you'll find step-by-step techniques and visuals to help you master the craft.

Whether it be with an intricately woven challah knot or an effortless, no-knead scone, every page of *The Bread Collection* brings you one step closer to your next bread-baking adventure. With this essential cookbook as your guide, take a deep dive into the world of dough and never look back.

quick BREADS

FAST, NO-FUSS QUICK BREADS FEATURE THE ALL-STARS OF THE BREAKFAST SPREAD, FROM SCONES TO MUFFINS TO BANANA BREAD

HONEY TEA LOAVES

This wholesome bread packs a subtle sweetness, making it perfect for breakfast or an afternoon snack. Substitute apple cider for bourbon for an even richer flavor.

Makes 4 mini loaves

2	cups (270 grams) chopped dried Calimyrna figs
1⅓	cups (449 grams) honey, divided
⅓	cup (80 grams) plus ¼ cup (60 grams) bourbon, divided
½	cup (113 grams) unsalted butter
⅓	cup (67 grams) granulated sugar
3	large eggs (150 grams)
5	cups (625 grams) cake flour
2	teaspoons (10 grams) baking powder
½	teaspoon (1.5 grams) kosher salt
¾	cup (180 grams) whole milk, divided
1¼	cups (150 grams) confectioners' sugar, sifted

Garnish: 1 cup (110 grams) sliced dried Calimyrna figs

1. In a medium saucepan, heat chopped figs, ⅓ cup (113 grams) honey, and ⅓ cup (80 grams) bourbon over medium heat until mixture begins to simmer. Remove from heat. Let stand until cool, about 30 minutes.

2. Preheat oven to 350°F (180°C). Butter and flour 4 (4½x2½-inch) mini loaf pans.

3. In the bowl of a stand mixer fitted with the paddle attachment, beat butter and granulated sugar at medium speed for 5 to 10 seconds. With mixer running, slowly add remaining 1 cup (336 grams) honey, beating until combined. Add eggs, one at a time, beating just until combined after each addition.

4. In a large bowl, whisk together flour, baking powder, and salt. With mixer on low speed, gradually add flour mixture to butter mixture alternately with ½ cup (120 grams) milk, beginning and ending with flour mixture, beating just until combined after each addition. Spoon half of batter into prepared pans; top with fig mixture. Spoon remaining batter over fig mixture.

5. Bake until golden brown and a wooden pick inserted in center comes out clean, about 35 minutes. Let cool in pans for 10 minutes. Run a knife around edges of loaves to loosen. Remove from pans, and let cool completely on a wire rack.

6. In a medium bowl, whisk together confectioners' sugar and remaining ¼ cup (60 grams) milk until smooth. Drizzle glaze over loaves.

7. In a small bowl, place sliced figs. In a small saucepan, heat remaining ¼ cup (60 grams) bourbon over medium heat until hot. Pour hot bourbon over sliced figs. Cover and let cool. Garnish cakes with bourbon figs. Wrap and freeze loaves for up to 2 weeks.

COCONUT POPOVERS WITH MANGO CHUTNEY

Cookbook author Ben Mims finds the coconut in these popovers lends a sweetness that pairs well with curries and other spicy dishes. Use the Mango Chutney as a spread on sandwiches with thick slices of Cheddar cheese, or mix it into mayonnaise as a dip for chicken fingers or a spread for deli sandwiches.

Makes 6

1¼   cups (300 grams) coconut water (fresh or bottled)
1   tablespoon (14 grams) unrefined coconut oil, melted
1   teaspoon (4 grams) coconut extract
3   large eggs (150 grams)
1   cup (125 grams) all-purpose flour
1   teaspoon (3 grams) kosher salt
2   tablespoons (30 grams) vegetable oil
Mango Chutney (recipe follows)

1. In a medium bowl, whisk together coconut water, melted coconut oil, coconut extract, and eggs until smooth. Add flour and salt; whisk until just combined (there will be some lumps). Cover with plastic wrap, and let stand at room temperature for at least 2 hours.
2. Preheat oven to 400°F (200°C). Pour 1 teaspoon (5 grams) vegetable oil into each cup of a 6-cup nonstick popover pan. Place popover pan on a rimmed baking sheet (to catch oil drips), and preheat in oven for 15 minutes. Remove pan from oven, and quickly pour batter into prepared cups, filling each about two-thirds full.
3. Bake until risen and golden brown, 30 to 35 minutes. Using a fork, poke holes in top of popovers to release steam. Unmold popovers, and serve hot with Mango Chutney.

MANGO CHUTNEY

Makes about 3 cups

1   pound (455 grams) ripe mango flesh, finely chopped
½   cup (75 grams) coconut sugar
½   cup (110 grams) firmly packed light brown sugar
½   cup (64 grams) raisins
½   cup (120 grams) apple cider vinegar
¼   cup (21 grams) finely shredded dried (desiccated) coconut
¼   cup (8 grams) minced peeled ginger
1½   tablespoons (22.5 grams) fresh lime juice
½   teaspoon (1 gram) chili powder
½   teaspoon (1.5 grams) kosher salt
¼   teaspoon ground black pepper
1   clove garlic (5 grams), minced
1   small red onion (30 grams), finely chopped

1. In a medium saucepan, bring all ingredients to a boil over medium-high heat. Reduce heat to medium-low, and cook, stirring occasionally, until reduced and thickened to a relish, 45 minutes to 1 hour. Remove from heat. Transfer chutney to glass jars, and seal while hot, or refrigerate in an airtight container for up to 2 weeks.

Recipe by Ben Mims / Photo by Mason + Dixon

CARAMELIZED ONION, POLENTA, AND FRESH HERB OLIVE OIL LOAF

This savory edition of our olive oil cake uses polenta to create a distinctly chewy texture similar to cornbread. Sweet caramelized onions and a bouquet of fresh herbs—rosemary, sage, and thyme—make this aromatic loaf a perfect accompaniment to dinner.

Makes 1 (9x5-inch) loaf

1	tablespoon (14 grams) unsalted butter
1	pound (455 grams) sweet yellow onions, sliced ¼ inch thick
1	tablespoon (15 grams) white balsamic vinegar
4	large eggs (200 grams)
¾	cup (168 grams) extra-virgin olive oil
¾	cup (180 grams) whole milk
2¼	cups (281 grams) all-purpose flour
⅓	cup (50 grams) fine-ground polenta
1	tablespoon (2 grams) chopped fresh thyme
1	tablespoon (2 grams) chopped fresh rosemary
1	tablespoon (2 grams) chopped fresh sage
2¼	teaspoons (11.25 grams) baking powder
1	teaspoon (3 grams) kosher salt
½	teaspoon (1 gram) ground black pepper

Crème fraîche, to serve
Garnish: extra-virgin olive oil, ground black pepper

1. Preheat oven to 350°F (180°C). Butter and flour a 9x5-inch loaf pan.
2. In a medium skillet, heat butter over medium heat. Add onions; cook until translucent and softened, about 10 minutes. Reduce heat to low, and cook until onions turn a very dark golden-brown color, about 2 hours, stirring every 10 minutes the first hour and every 5 minutes the second hour. (Be careful not to let onions burn.) When nearing the end of the second hour, stir and scrape any browned bits from bottom of pan. Increase heat to medium, and stir in vinegar, scraping browned bits from bottom of pan. Stir onions, and set aside to let cool.
3. Place eggs in the bowl of a stand mixer fitted with the whisk attachment. With mixer on high speed, add oil in a slow, steady stream until combined. Add milk, beating until combined.
4. In a medium bowl, whisk together flour, polenta, thyme, rosemary, sage, baking powder, salt, and pepper. With mixer on low speed, gradually add flour mixture to egg mixture, beating until combined. Fold in caramelized onions. Pour batter into prepared pan.
5. Bake until a wooden pick inserted in center comes out clean, 50 to 55 minutes. Let cool in pan for 5 minutes. Remove from pan, and let cool completely on a wire rack. Serve with crème fraîche, and garnish with a drizzle of olive oil and a sprinkle of pepper, if desired. Store at room temperature wrapped in foil.

STRAWBERRY CUCUMBER BREAD

Ripe strawberries and fresh cucumbers are stirred into the batter to create a bread that's light enough for a morning snack but sweet enough to be an afternoon treat.

Makes 1 (9x5-inch) loaf

½   cup (160 grams) strawberry preserves
1   tablespoon (8 grams) cornstarch
1   tablespoon (15 grams) fresh lemon juice
½   cup (113 grams) clarified butter, softened
1   cup (200 grams) granulated sugar
2   large eggs (100 grams)
1   teaspoon (4 grams) vanilla extract
¼   teaspoon (1 gram) almond extract
2   cups (250 grams) all-purpose flour
1   teaspoon (5 grams) baking powder
½   teaspoon (2.5 grams) baking soda
½   teaspoon (1.5 grams) kosher salt
2   cups (250 grams) grated and well-drained cucumber
½   cup (57 grams) chopped walnuts
½   cup (85 grams) sliced fresh strawberries, divided

1. In a small saucepan, cook strawberry preserves, cornstarch, and lemon juice over medium heat until slightly thickened, about 5 minutes. Let cool completely.
2. Preheat oven to 325°F (170°C). Butter and flour a 9x5-inch loaf pan.
3. In the bowl of a stand mixer fitted with the paddle attachment, beat clarified butter and sugar at medium speed until fluffy, 3 to 4 minutes, stopping to scrape sides of bowl. Add eggs, one at a time, beating well after each addition. Beat in extracts.
4. In a medium bowl, whisk together flour, baking powder, baking soda, and salt. With mixer on low speed, gradually add flour mixture to butter mixture, beating just until combined. Stir in cucumber, walnuts, and ¼ cup (42.5 grams) strawberries. Spoon half of batter into prepared pan; top with strawberry preserves mixture. Add remaining batter, and top with remaining ¼ cup (42.5 grams) strawberries.
5. Bake until a wooden pick inserted in center comes out clean, 1 hour to 1 hour and 15 minutes. Let cool in pan for 10 minutes. Remove from pan, and let cool completely on a wire rack. Wrap and store at room temperature for up to 1 week.

COCONUT AND EARL GREY SCONES

Floral notes of orange and bitter black tea pair well with the rich aroma of coconut in these scones from cookbook author Ben Mims. Even though pieces of coconut, its milk, and oil are used here, the subtle flavor of coconut needs the boost of extract for its full flavor to come through. The coconut sugar sprinkled on top is too savory to use as the sweetener in the scones, but it offers the perfect amount of crunch and toasted coconut aroma when sprinkled on top. If you can't find coconut sugar, you can use granulated or light brown sugar instead.

Makes 8

2	cups (480 grams) unsweetened canned coconut milk
2	tablespoons (12 grams) finely ground Earl Grey tea
1	teaspoon (4 grams) coconut extract
1	cup (84 grams) unsweetened flaked coconut
5	cups (625 grams) all-purpose flour
½	cup (100 grams) granulated sugar
1	tablespoon plus 2 teaspoons (25 grams) baking powder
2½	teaspoons (7.5 grams) kosher salt
⅓	cup (75 grams) unrefined coconut oil, frozen
½	cup (113 grams) cold unsalted butter, cubed

Heavy whipping cream, for brushing
Garnish: coconut sugar

1. In a small saucepan, bring coconut milk and tea to a boil over medium-high heat. Remove from heat, and stir in coconut extract. Let cool completely. Refrigerate tea-infused milk until chilled; strain, discarding solids.

2. Preheat oven to 350°F (180°C). Spread coconut flakes on a baking sheet, and bake until lightly golden brown, about 8 minutes. Transfer coconut to a bowl, and let cool completely.

3. In a large bowl, whisk together flour, granulated sugar, baking powder, and salt. Finely grate frozen coconut oil with a serrated knife into ¼-inch pieces; add to dry ingredients along with cold butter, and rub into dry ingredients quickly with your fingers until butter looks like pea-size crumbles. Stir in toasted coconut; add chilled tea milk, and stir with a fork until a dough forms. Transfer dough to a lightly floured surface, and pat into a 9-inch circle, about 1 inch thick. Cut into 8 wedges, and transfer to a parchment paper-lined baking sheet. Freeze for at least 1 hour or up to 1 week.

4. Preheat oven to 350°F (180°C).

5. Brush top of frozen scones with cream, and garnish each with a hefty pinch of coconut sugar, if desired.

6. Bake until risen and deep golden brown, 25 to 35 minutes.

Recipe by Ben Mims / Photo by Mason + Dixon

ITALIAN PLUM-AND-PARMESAN SCONES

Italian plums are most commonly associated with their dried counterpart prunes, but they are great for baking thanks to a concentrated sweetness and easy-to-remove pit. Prepare for some magic as these scones bake—the yellow-fleshed plums turn a hot fuchsia.

Makes 8

2½   cups (313 grams) all-purpose flour
¾   cup (75 grams) freshly grated Parmigiano-Reggiano cheese
3   tablespoons (36 grams) granulated sugar
1   tablespoon (15 grams) baking powder
1   teaspoon (3 grams) kosher salt
½   teaspoon (1 gram) ground black pepper
½   cup (113 grams) cold unsalted butter, cubed
1¼   cups (219 grams) finely chopped Italian plums
½   cup (120 grams) heavy whipping cream
½   cup (120 grams) whole buttermilk
1   large egg (50 grams), well beaten
½   cup (113 grams) unsalted butter, softened
3   tablespoons (63 grams) honey

1. Preheat oven to 425°F (220°C). Line a baking sheet with parchment paper.
2. In a large bowl, stir together flour, cheese, sugar, baking powder, salt, and pepper. Using a pastry blender, cut in cold butter until mixture is crumbly. Freeze for 15 minutes.
3. Fold plums into flour mixture. Add cream and buttermilk, stirring with a fork just until dry ingredients are moistened. Gather mixture together, and gently knead into a ball.
4. Turn out dough onto prepared pan, and pat into an 8-inch circle. Cut into 8 wedges; gently separate wedges about ½ inch apart. Brush with egg. Sprinkle with additional cheese and pepper, if desired.
5. Bake until golden and centers are firm, 22 to 25 minutes. Let cool on a wire rack for 10 minutes.
6. In a small bowl, stir together butter and honey. Season with salt and pepper to taste. Serve scones warm with butter mixture.

Recipe by Marian Cooper Cairns / Photo by Matt Armendariz

WALNUT GOLDEN RAISIN SODA BREAD

Earthy walnuts and sweet golden raisins add texture and a hint of sweetness to this classic, which gets extra depth from whole wheat flour as well as sunflower and pumpkin seeds.

Makes 1 (10-inch) boule

4½	cups (563 grams) plus 1 teaspoon (3 grams) all-purpose flour, divided
1½	cups (195 grams) whole wheat flour
½	cup (100 grams) granulated sugar
1	tablespoon (15 grams) baking soda
2	teaspoons (6 grams) kosher salt
1½	cups (192 grams) golden raisins
1	cup (113 grams) chopped walnuts
2	cups plus 2 tablespoons (510 grams) whole buttermilk
6	tablespoons (84 grams) unsalted butter, melted
1	tablespoon (9 grams) sunflower seeds
1	teaspoon (3 grams) pumpkin seeds

1. Preheat oven to 425°F (220°C). Butter and flour a 10-inch cast-iron skillet.

2. In a large bowl, whisk together 4½ cups (563 grams) all-purpose flour, whole wheat flour, sugar, baking soda, and salt. Stir in raisins and walnuts. Gradually add buttermilk and melted butter, stirring just until dry ingredients are moistened. Gently knead dough 3 to 4 times until ingredients are combined.

3. On a lightly floured surface, shape dough into a ball. Press into prepared pan. Sprinkle with sunflower seeds, pumpkin seeds, and remaining 1 teaspoon (3 grams) all-purpose flour. With a sharp knife, score a shallow "X" on top of dough.

4. Bake until golden brown and a wooden pick inserted in center comes out clean, 35 to 40 minutes, loosely covering with foil to prevent excess browning, if necessary. Let cool in pan for 10 minutes.

ROSEMARY PARMESAN SODA BREAD

The divine pairing of fresh Parmesan and rosemary strikes a perfect balance between the simple ingredients and deliciously complex flavors in this savory take on tradition.

Makes 1 (8-inch) boule

4½   cups (563 grams) all-purpose flour
2   tablespoons (24 grams) granulated sugar
4   teaspoons (2.5 grams) chopped fresh rosemary
2   teaspoons (6 grams) kosher salt
1½   teaspoons (7.5 grams) baking soda
¼   teaspoon ground black pepper
1¼   cups (125 grams) grated Parmesan cheese
1¾   cups (420 grams) whole buttermilk
¼   cup (57 grams) unsalted butter, melted
1   large egg (50 grams)
1½   teaspoons (4.5 grams) flaked sea salt

1. Preheat oven to 425°F (220°C). Line a rimmed baking sheet with parchment paper.
2. In a large bowl, whisk together flour, sugar, rosemary, kosher salt, baking soda, and pepper. Stir in cheese.
3. In a medium bowl, whisk together buttermilk, melted butter, and egg. Gradually add buttermilk mixture to flour mixture, stirring just until dry ingredients are moistened. Knead dough just until ingredients are combined.
4. On a lightly floured surface, shape dough into a ball. Place on prepared pan, pressing to flatten dough into a 7-inch circle, 1½ inches thick. With a sharp knife, score a shallow "X" on top of dough. Sprinkle with flaked salt.
5. Bake until golden brown and a wooden pick inserted in center comes out clean, 35 to 40 minutes, loosely covering with foil to prevent excess browning, if necessary. Let cool on pan for 10 minutes.

ZUCCHINI BANANA BREAD

Zucchini brings extra moisture to this classic quick bread, making for a more tender crumb than you'd find in standard banana bread. A medley of warm spices complements both the banana and summer squash beautifully.

Makes 1 (9x5-inch) loaf

½   cup (113 grams) unsalted butter, softened
¾   cup (150 grams) granulated sugar
2   large eggs (100 grams)
2   cups (250 grams) all-purpose flour
1   teaspoon (5 grams) baking powder
1   teaspoon (5 grams) baking soda
1   teaspoon (3 grams) kosher salt
½   teaspoon (1 gram) ground cinnamon
¼   teaspoon ground nutmeg
1½   cups (341 grams) mashed ripe banana (about 3 medium)
1   cup (110 grams) grated zucchini
1   teaspoon (4 grams) vanilla extract
1   banana (124 grams), halved lengthwise
1   teaspoon (4 grams) produce protector*
1   teaspoon (5 grams) water

1. Preheat oven to 350°F (180°C). Butter and flour bottom of a 9x5-inch loaf pan.
2. In the bowl of a stand mixer fitted with the paddle attachment, beat butter and sugar at medium speed until fluffy, 3 to 4 minutes, stopping to scrape sides of bowl. Add eggs, one at a time, beating well after each addition.
3. In a medium bowl, whisk together flour, baking powder, baking soda, salt, cinnamon, and nutmeg. With mixer on low speed, gradually add flour mixture to butter mixture, beating just until combined. Beat in mashed banana, zucchini, and vanilla. Spoon batter into prepared pan, smoothing top with an offset spatula. Place banana halves, cut side up, on top of batter.
4. In a small bowl, combine produce protector and 1 teaspoon (5 grams) water. Brush mixture on cut side of banana halves to retain color.
5. Bake until a wooden pick inserted in center comes out clean, about 1 hour and 10 minutes. Let cool in pan for 10 minutes. Remove from pan, and let cool completely on a wire rack. Store in an airtight container at room temperature for up to 3 days.

We used Ball Fruit-Fresh Produce Protector.

PRO TIP
If using zucchini out of season, gently press grated zucchini with paper towels to soak up excess moisture before using.

GLUTEN-FREE BANANA BREAD

Hazelnut and almond flours give this Gluten-Free Banana Bread a complex, earthy flavor. We love the addition of chopped hazelnuts, in lieu of pecans or walnuts, for a twist on the original.

Makes 1 (9x5-inch) loaf

1½   cups plus 2 tablespoons (222 grams) gluten-free flour blend*, divided
¼   cup (28 grams) chopped skinned hazelnuts
1   cup (200 grams) plus 2 tablespoons (24 grams) granulated sugar, divided
½   cup (110 grams) plus 2 tablespoons (28 grams) firmly packed light brown sugar, divided
1¼   teaspoons (3 grams) kosher salt, divided
½   cup (113 grams) unsalted butter, melted and divided
1¼   cups (120 grams) almond flour
1¼   cups (120 grams) hazelnut flour
1   tablespoon (15 grams) baking powder
1   teaspoon (2 grams) ground cinnamon
1   teaspoon grated fresh nutmeg
4   medium very ripe bananas (493 grams), mashed
¾   cup (180 grams) sour cream
3   tablespoons (63 grams) honey
1   large egg (50 grams)
1   teaspoon (6 grams) vanilla bean paste

1. Preheat oven to 350°F (180°C). Spray a 9x5-inch loaf pan with cooking spray, and line pan with parchment paper.

2. In a medium bowl, whisk together ¼ cup plus 2 tablespoons (52 grams) gluten-free flour blend, hazelnuts, 2 tablespoons (24 grams) granulated sugar, 2 tablespoons (28 grams) brown sugar, and ¼ teaspoon salt. Drizzle with ¼ cup (56.5 grams) melted butter, and stir with a wooden spoon until combined. Crumble with your fingertips until desired consistency is reached. Set aside.

3. In a large bowl, whisk together flours, baking powder, cinnamon, nutmeg, remaining 1¼ cups (170 grams) gluten-free flour blend, and remaining 1 teaspoon (3 grams) salt.

4. In a medium bowl, combine banana, sour cream, honey, egg, vanilla bean paste, remaining 1 cup (200 grams) granulated sugar, remaining ½ cup (110 grams) brown sugar, and remaining ¼ cup (56.5 grams) melted butter. Make a well in center of flour mixture; fold in banana mixture until well combined. Pour mixture into prepared pan, and smooth top with a spatula. Sprinkle with streusel.

5. Bake until a wooden pick inserted in center comes out clean, 55 minutes to 1 hour and 15 minutes, loosely covering with foil halfway through baking to prevent excess browning, if necessary.

*We used Cup4Cup.

RHUBARB-GINGER MUFFINS WITH RHUBARB-VANILLA BEAN STREUSEL

We love the tiny bursts of red that diced rhubarb brings to this tender treat's batter. Ginger lends just the right amount of kick, and a vanilla bean streusel topping packs the perfect crunch.

Makes 18

2	cups (250 grams) all-purpose flour
1	cup (200 grams) granulated sugar
1	teaspoon (5 grams) baking powder
1	teaspoon (2 grams) ground ginger
1	teaspoon grated fresh nutmeg
½	teaspoon (2.5 grams) baking soda
½	teaspoon (1.5 grams) kosher salt
1½	cups (150 grams) diced rhubarb
3	large eggs (150 grams)
1	cup (240 grams) sour cream
½	cup (120 grams) whole buttermilk
¼	cup (57 grams) unsalted butter, melted and slightly cooled
1	teaspoon (6 grams) vanilla bean paste
1	tablespoon (3 grams) lemon zest

Rhubarb-Vanilla Bean Streusel (recipe follows)

1. Preheat oven to 375°F (190°C). Butter and flour 18 muffin cups, or line with paper liners.

2. In a large bowl, whisk together flour, sugar, baking powder, ginger, nutmeg, baking soda, and salt. Stir in rhubarb.

3. In a medium bowl, whisk together eggs, sour cream, buttermilk, melted butter, vanilla bean paste, and zest. Fold egg mixture into flour mixture, stirring just until combined. Divide batter among prepared muffin cups. Top with Rhubarb-Vanilla Bean Streusel.

4. Bake until a wooden pick inserted in center comes out clean, 20 to 30 minutes. Let cool in pans for 5 minutes. Serve warm or at room temperature.

RHUBARB-VANILLA BEAN STREUSEL

Makes 2 cups

¾	cup (94 grams) all-purpose flour
¼	cup (50 grams) granulated sugar
¼	cup (55 grams) firmly packed light brown sugar
½	teaspoon (1.5 grams) kosher salt
½	teaspoon (1 gram) ground ginger
1	vanilla bean, split lengthwise, seeds scraped and reserved
¼	cup (57 grams) unsalted butter, melted
½	cup (50 grams) finely diced rhubarb

1. In a medium bowl, whisk together flour, sugars, salt, ginger, and reserved vanilla bean seeds. Drizzle with melted butter. Using a wooden spoon, stir to combine. Crumble with your fingertips until desired consistency is reached. Fold in rhubarb.

Photo by Stephen DeVries

PEAR-WALNUT MUFFINS WITH VANILLA BEAN-GINGER STREUSEL

Simultaneously airy and decadent, these muffins are the perfect treat for cool mornings. The vanilla bean in the streusel softens the punch of the ginger to give a rich sweetness with a mellow bite.

Makes about 24

2	cups (250 grams) all-purpose flour
1½	cups (337.5 grams) diced pear
1	cup (200 grams) granulated sugar
1	cup (113 grams) chopped walnuts
1	teaspoon (5 grams) baking powder
1	teaspoon (2 grams) ground ginger
1	teaspoon (2 grams) ground cinnamon
1	teaspoon grated fresh nutmeg
½	teaspoon (2.5 grams) baking soda
½	teaspoon (1.5 grams) kosher salt
3	large eggs (150 grams)
1	cup (240 grams) sour cream
½	cup (120 grams) whole buttermilk
¼	cup (57 grams) unsalted butter, melted and slightly cooled
1	teaspoon (6 grams) vanilla bean paste

Vanilla Bean-Ginger Streusel (recipe follows)

1. Preheat oven to 375°F (190°C). Butter and flour 2 (12-cup) muffin pans, or line with paper liners.

2. In a large bowl, whisk together flour, pear, sugar, walnuts, baking powder, ginger, cinnamon, nutmeg, baking soda, and salt.

3. In a medium bowl, whisk together eggs, sour cream, buttermilk, melted butter, and vanilla bean paste. Fold egg mixture into flour mixture just until combined. Divide batter among prepared muffin cups. Top with Vanilla Bean-Ginger Streusel.

4. Bake until a wooden pick inserted in center comes out clean, 20 to 25 minutes. Let cool in pans for 5 minutes. Serve warm or at room temperature.

VANILLA BEAN-GINGER STREUSEL

Makes 1½ cups

¾	cup (94 grams) all-purpose flour
¼	cup (50 grams) granulated sugar
¼	cup (55 grams) firmly packed light brown sugar
½	teaspoon (1.5 grams) kosher salt
½	teaspoon (1 gram) ground ginger
1	vanilla bean, split lengthwise, seeds scraped and reserved
¼	cup (57 grams) unsalted butter, melted

1. In a medium bowl, whisk together flour, sugars, salt, ginger, and reserved vanilla bean seeds. Drizzle with melted butter, and stir with a wooden spoon until combined. Crumble with your fingertips until desired consistency is reached.

QUICK BREADS   **37**

STRAWBERRY-BALSAMIC MUFFINS

Sweet strawberries and tangy balsamic vinegar are a match made in heaven. These muffins take this combo to an entirely new level.

Makes 8

1   cup (200 grams) granulated sugar
1   cup (240 grams) sour cream
3   large eggs (150 grams)
½   cup (120 grams) fresh orange juice
2¾   cups (344 grams) all-purpose flour
2   teaspoons (10 grams) baking powder
1   teaspoon (3 grams) kosher salt
½   cup (112 grams) vegetable oil
1½   cups (255 grams) chopped fresh strawberries
½   cup (120 grams) Balsamic Reduction (recipe follows)
½   cup (100 grams) turbinado sugar

1. Preheat oven to 425°F (220°C). Line 8 jumbo muffin cups with parchment or paper liners, or spray with cooking spray.
2. In the bowl of a stand mixer fitted with the whisk attachment, beat granulated sugar, sour cream, eggs, and orange juice at medium speed until well combined, 3 to 4 minutes, stopping to scrape sides of bowl.
3. In a medium bowl, whisk together flour, baking powder, and salt. With mixer on low speed, gradually add flour mixture to sugar mixture, beating until combined. With mixer running, add oil in a slow, steady stream until combined. Fold in strawberries.
4. Spoon batter into prepared muffin cups. Top each muffin with 1 tablespoon (15 grams) Balsamic Reduction, and use a wooden pick to swirl. Sprinkle with turbinado sugar.
5. Bake for 5 minutes. Reduce oven temperature to 350°F (180°C), and bake until golden brown and a wooden pick inserted in center comes out clean, 25 to 30 minutes more. Let cool in pans for 5 minutes. Serve warm or at room temperature.

BALSAMIC REDUCTION
Makes about ¾ cup

1   cup (240 grams) high-quality balsamic vinegar

1. In a small saucepan, bring balsamic vinegar to a boil over medium-high heat. Reduce heat to medium, and simmer until vinegar coats the back of a spoon and is reduced to about ¾ cup. Let cool completely. Cover and refrigerate for up to 1 month.

Note: *We styled this photo in a regular muffin tin, but you need to bake them in a jumbo muffin tin.*

Photo by Stephen DeVries

BEET AND GOAT CHEESE MUFFINS WITH ORANGE STREUSEL

Your favorite salad gets a sweet makeover in muffin form. Beet Purée adds moisture and tenderness. Goat cheese serves as a salty juxtaposition and lets the natural sweetness of the beets shine through.

Makes 8

4	ounces (115 grams) crumbled goat cheese
1⅔	cups (208 grams) all-purpose flour
1	cup (200 grams) granulated sugar
2	tablespoons (6 grams) orange zest
2	teaspoons (10 grams) baking powder
1	teaspoon (3 grams) kosher salt
1	cup (240 grams) sour cream
3	large eggs (150 grams)
	Beet Purée (recipe follows)
½	cup (112 grams) vegetable oil
1	cup (113 grams) chopped pecans
	Orange Streusel (recipe follows)

1. Preheat oven to 350°F (180°C). Line 8 jumbo muffin cups with parchment or paper liners, or spray with cooking spray.
2. In a large bowl, whisk together goat cheese, flour, sugar, zest, baking powder, and salt. In a medium bowl, whisk together sour cream, eggs, Beet Purée, and oil. Make a well in center of goat cheese mixture; add sour cream mixture, stirring just until moistened. Fold in pecans. Spoon batter into prepared muffin cups. Top with Orange Streusel.
3. Bake until a wooden pick inserted in center comes out clean, 25 to 30 minutes. Let cool in pans for 5 minutes. Serve warm or at room temperature.

BEET PURÉE
Makes ½ cup

1	tablespoon (14 grams) olive oil
2	large beets (185 grams), greens trimmed

1. Preheat oven to 400°F (200°C). Drizzle oil over beets, and wrap loosely in foil. Bake until beets are fork tender, 45 minutes to 1 hour.
2. When cool enough to handle, peel beets, and transfer to the work bowl of a food processor. Process until beets are puréed, 2 to 3 minutes.

ORANGE STREUSEL
Makes 2½ cups

1⅔	cups (208 grams) all-purpose flour
⅓	cup (67 grams) granulated sugar
⅓	cup (73 grams) firmly packed light brown sugar
2	tablespoons (6 grams) orange zest
½	teaspoon (1.5 grams) kosher salt
½	cup (113 grams) unsalted butter, melted

1. In a small bowl, whisk together flour, sugars, zest, and salt. Drizzle with melted butter, and stir with a wooden spoon until combined. Crumble with your fingertips until desired consistency is reached.

Photo by Stephen DeVries

BANANA CHOCOLATE ESPRESSO SWIRL MUFFINS

We're not sure if these muffins are breakfast or dessert, but we promise not to judge if you eat one (OK, three) hot out of the oven. (They're THAT good.)

Makes 8

1   cup (170 grams) semisweet chocolate morsels
1½   tablespoons (9 grams) espresso powder
2¼   cups (281 grams) all-purpose flour
¾   cup (150 grams) granulated sugar
1   teaspoon (5 grams) baking soda
½   teaspoon (1.5 grams) kosher salt
1   teaspoon (2 grams) ground cinnamon
½   teaspoon grated fresh nutmeg
1½   cups (341 grams) mashed banana (about 3 medium bananas)
2   large eggs (100 grams)
½   cup (112 grams) vegetable oil
¼   cup (60 grams) whole buttermilk
1   tablespoon (21 grams) unsulphered molasses
1   teaspoon (4 grams) vanilla extract

1. Preheat oven to 350°F (180°C). Line 8 jumbo muffin cups with parchment or paper liners, or spray with cooking spray.
2. In the top of a double boiler, combine chocolate and espresso powder. Cook over simmering water until chocolate is melted. Remove from heat, and let cool.
3. In a large bowl, whisk together flour, sugar, baking soda, salt, cinnamon, and nutmeg. In a medium bowl, whisk together banana, eggs, oil, buttermilk, molasses, and vanilla. Make a well in center of flour mixture; add banana mixture, stirring just until moistened. Spoon 1½ cups (330 grams) batter into a small bowl, and stir in chocolate-espresso mixture.
4. Spoon banana batter into prepared muffin cups, filling two-thirds full. Using the back of a spoon, make a shallow trench in center of each muffin cup. Spoon in chocolate-espresso batter, and swirl with a wooden pick.
5. Bake until a wooden pick inserted in center comes out clean, 25 to 30 minutes. Let cool in pans for 5 minutes. Serve warm or at room temperature.

Photo by Stephen DeVries

BLUEBERRY-CORNMEAL MUFFINS WITH THYME GLAZE

Sometimes it's the unexpected flavor profiles that become our favorites. Corn and thyme might not be the first things you think of when you think "blueberry muffin," but trust us, this combination is killer.

Makes 8

½ cup (113 grams) unsalted butter, softened
1⅓ cups (293 grams) firmly packed light brown sugar
2 large eggs (100 grams)
1 teaspoon (4 grams) vanilla extract
1⅔ cups (209 grams) all-purpose flour
1 cup (150 grams) yellow cornmeal
1 teaspoon (5 grams) baking powder
1 teaspoon (5 grams) baking soda
½ teaspoon (1.5 grams) kosher salt
1 cup (240 grams) whole buttermilk
1½ cups (255 grams) fresh blueberries
Thyme Glaze (recipe follows)

1. Preheat oven to 425°F (220°C). Line 8 jumbo muffin cups with parchment or paper liners, or spray with cooking spray.
2. In the bowl of a stand mixer fitted with the paddle attachment, beat butter and brown sugar at medium speed until fluffy, 3 to 4 minutes, stopping to scrape sides of bowl. Add eggs, one at a time, beating well after each addition. Beat in vanilla.
3. In a medium bowl, whisk together flour, cornmeal, baking powder, baking soda, and salt. With mixer on low speed, gradually add flour mixture to butter mixture alternately with buttermilk, beginning and ending with flour mixture, beating just until combined after each addition. Fold in blueberries. Spoon batter into prepared muffin cups.
4. Bake for 5 minutes. Reduce oven temperature to 350°F (180°C), and bake until golden brown and a wooden pick inserted in center comes out clean, 25 to 30 minutes more. Let cool in pans for 5 minutes. Drizzle with Thyme Glaze, and serve warm or at room temperature.

THYME GLAZE

Makes ⅓ cup

1¼ cups (150 grams) confectioners' sugar
Thyme Syrup (recipe follows)

1. In a small bowl, whisk together confectioners' sugar and Thyme Syrup until smooth.

THYME SYRUP

Makes ¼ cup

¼ cup (50 grams) granulated sugar
¼ cup (60 grams) water
4 sprigs fresh thyme

1. In a small saucepan, bring all ingredients to a boil over medium-high heat, stirring occasionally, until sugar is dissolved, about 5 minutes. Remove from heat, and let cool completely. Discard thyme sprigs before using.

Photo by Stephen DeVries

VANILLA BEAN AND CARDAMOM SCONES WITH VANILLA BEAN GLAZE

We spiced up the classic, soothing vanilla bean scone with a touch of cardamom.

Makes 8

2   cups (250 grams) all-purpose flour
½   cup (100 grams) granulated sugar, divided
1   tablespoon (15 grams) baking powder
2   teaspoons (6 grams) kosher salt
½   teaspoon (1 gram) ground cardamom
2   vanilla beans, split lengthwise, seeds scraped and reserved, divided
5   tablespoons (70 grams) cold unsalted butter, cubed
1   cup (240 grams) plus 1 teaspoon (5 grams) heavy whipping cream, divided
1   large egg (50 grams)
¼   cup (60 grams) water
½   cup (60 grams) confectioners' sugar

1. Preheat oven to 425°F (220°C). Butter and flour an 8-inch round cake pan. Line a baking sheet with parchment paper.
2. In the work bowl of a food processor, place flour, ¼ cup (50 grams) granulated sugar, baking powder, salt, cardamom, and half of vanilla bean seeds; pulse until combined. Add cold butter, and pulse until mixture is crumbly.

3. Transfer dough to a large bowl; fold in 1 cup (240 grams) cream until combined. Turn out dough onto a lightly floured surface, and knead briefly, just until dough comes together. Press dough into prepared cake pan. Turn out, and using a sharp knife or bench scraper, cut into 8 wedges. Transfer wedges to prepared baking sheet.
4. In a small bowl, whisk together egg and remaining 1 teaspoon (5 grams) cream. Brush top of scones with egg wash.
5. Bake until golden brown, 12 to 15 minutes.
6. In a small saucepan, bring ¼ cup (60 grams) water, remaining ¼ cup (50 grams) granulated sugar, and 1 vanilla bean and remaining seeds to a boil over medium-high heat. Boil, stirring occasionally, until sugar is dissolved, about 5 minutes. Remove from heat, and let cool completely. Strain mixture through a fine-mesh sieve, discarding solids.
7. In a small bowl, whisk together 2 tablespoons vanilla syrup and confectioners' sugar until smooth. Drizzle over warm scones.

PEAR CHAI SPICED SCONES WITH SPICED PEAR GLAZE

Baked with an aromatic Indian spice and topped with a sweet pear drizzle, these scones are bursting with flavor.

Makes 8

2   cups (250 grams) all-purpose flour
½   cup (100 grams) granulated sugar, divided
1   tablespoon (15 grams) baking powder
2   teaspoons (6 grams) kosher salt
1   teaspoon (2 grams) ground cinnamon
1   teaspoon (2 grams) ground ginger
½   teaspoon grated fresh nutmeg
¼   teaspoon ground cardamom
¼   teaspoon ground black pepper
5   tablespoons (70 grams) cold unsalted butter, cubed
2   small pears (200 grams), cored and chopped
1   cup (240 grams) plus 1 teaspoon (5 grams) heavy whipping
      cream, divided
1   large egg (50 grams)
¼   cup (60 grams) water
1   pear (100 grams), sliced
1   cinnamon stick
1   star anise (2 grams)
½   cup (60 grams) confectioners' sugar

1. Preheat oven to 425°F (220°C). Butter and flour an 8-inch round cake pan. Line a baking sheet with parchment paper.
2. In the work bowl of a food processor, place flour, ¼ cup (50 grams) granulated sugar, baking powder, salt, cinnamon, ginger, nutmeg, cardamom, and pepper; pulse until combined. Add cold butter, and pulse until mixture is crumbly.
3. Transfer dough to a large bowl; fold in chopped pears and 1 cup (240 grams) cream until combined. Turn out dough onto a lightly floured surface, and knead briefly, just until dough comes together. Press dough into prepared cake pan. Turn out, and using a sharp knife or bench scraper, cut into 8 wedges. Transfer wedges to prepared baking sheet.
4. In a small bowl, whisk together egg and remaining 1 teaspoon (5 grams) cream. Brush top of scones with egg wash.
5. Bake until golden brown, 12 to 16 minutes.
6. In a small saucepan, bring ¼ cup (60 grams) water, sliced pear, cinnamon stick, star anise, and remaining ¼ cup (50 grams) granulated sugar to a boil over medium-high heat, stirring occasionally, until sugar is dissolved, about 5 minutes. Remove from heat, and let cool completely. Strain mixture through a fine-mesh sieve, discarding solids.
7. In a small bowl, whisk together 2 tablespoons spiced pear syrup and confectioners' sugar until smooth. Drizzle over warm scones.

BLACK PEPPER, CHEDDAR, AND PECAN SCONES

Sharp Cheddar cheese pairs perfectly with the nuttiness of pecans in these savory scones. So delicious, they don't even need a glaze.

Makes 8

2　cups (250 grams) all-purpose flour
2　tablespoons (24 grams) granulated sugar
1　tablespoon (15 grams) baking powder
2　teaspoons (6 grams) kosher salt
2 to 3 teaspoons (4 to 6 grams) ground black pepper, according to taste
5　tablespoons (70 grams) cold unsalted butter, cubed
1½　cups (150 grams) shredded Cheddar cheese
½　cup (57 grams) toasted chopped pecans
1　cup (240 grams) plus 1 teaspoon (5 grams) heavy whipping cream, divided
1　large egg (50 grams)
Ground black pepper and Maldon sea salt, for finishing (optional)

1. Preheat oven to 425°F (220°C). Butter and flour an 8-inch round cake pan. Line a baking sheet with parchment paper.
2. In the work bowl of a food processor, place flour, sugar, baking powder, salt, and pepper; pulse until combined. Add cold butter, and pulse until mixture is crumbly.
3. Transfer dough to a large bowl; fold in Cheddar, pecans, and 1 cup (240 grams) cream until combined. Turn out dough onto a lightly floured surface, and knead briefly, just until dough comes together. Press dough into prepared cake pan. Turn out, and using a sharp knife or bench scraper, cut into 8 wedges. Transfer wedges to prepared baking sheet.
4. In a small bowl, whisk together egg and remaining 1 teaspoon (5 grams) cream. Brush top of scones with egg wash, and sprinkle with pepper and sea salt, if desired.
5. Bake until golden brown, 12 to 15 minutes. Serve warm.

SWEET POTATO-SAGE SCONES WITH VANILLA BEAN MAPLE GLAZE

Tender and lovely in a warm shade of orange, these root vegetable-packed scones are not only beautiful but nutritious.

Makes 6

1	large sweet potato (500 grams)
2	cups (250 grams) all-purpose flour
¼	cup (50 grams) granulated sugar
¼	cup (8 grams) chopped fresh sage
1	tablespoon (15 grams) baking powder
½	teaspoon (1.5 grams) kosher salt
1	teaspoon (2 grams) ground cinnamon
½	teaspoon grated fresh nutmeg
½	cup (113 grams) cold unsalted butter, cubed
¾	cup (180 grams) plus 1 teaspoon (5 grams) heavy whipping cream, divided
1	large egg (50 grams)
½	cup (170 grams) maple syrup
½	vanilla bean, split lengthwise, seeds scraped and reserved
1	cup (120 grams) confectioners' sugar

1. Preheat oven to 400°F (200°C). Butter and flour an 8-inch round cake pan. Line a baking sheet with foil.

2. Scrub sweet potato, pat dry, and pierce several times with a fork. Bake until tender, about 40 minutes. Let cool for 10 minutes; peel.

Using a fork, mash pulp. Cover and refrigerate for 20 minutes. Increase oven temperature to 425°F (220°C).

3. In the work bowl of a food processor, place flour, granulated sugar, sage, baking powder, salt, cinnamon, and nutmeg; pulse until combined. Add cold butter, and pulse until mixture is crumbly. Transfer mixture to a medium bowl; stir in mashed sweet potato and ¾ cup (180 grams) cream.

4. Turn out dough onto a lightly floured surface, and knead briefly, just until dough comes together. Press dough into prepared cake pan. Turn out, and using a sharp knife or bench scraper, cut into 8 wedges. Transfer wedges to prepared baking sheet.

5. In a small bowl, whisk together egg and remaining 1 teaspoon (5 grams) cream. Brush top of scones with egg wash.

6. Bake until golden brown, 12 to 15 minutes.

7. In a small saucepan, heat maple syrup and vanilla bean and reserved seeds over low heat. Cook until warm and fragrant (do not boil). Remove from heat, and let cool slightly. Strain mixture through a fine-mesh sieve, discarding solids. Whisk in confectioners' sugar until smooth. Drizzle over warm scones.

twist BREADS

FROM BRAIDED WREATH BREADS TO AN ANYTIME CINNAMON SWIRL LOAF, THESE BEAUTIFULLY FORMED LOAVES OF TWISTED DOUGH ARE A TRIUMPH FOR THE EYES AND TASTE BUDS

BRAIDED MAZANEC

With amaretto-soaked golden raisins and Marzipan, the Czech Republic's mazanec is an Easter bread all-star.

Makes 2 (12-inch) braids

½ cup (120 grams) amaretto
¼ cup (60 grams) water
2 cups (256 grams) golden raisins
1¼ cups (300 grams) warm whole milk (105°F/41°C to 110°F/43°C)
4½ teaspoons (14 grams) active dry yeast
½ cup (120 grams) heavy whipping cream
¼ cup (60 grams) freshly squeezed orange juice, strained
1 cup (200 grams) granulated sugar
3 large eggs (150 grams), divided
2 large egg yolks (37 grams)
2½ teaspoons (7.5 grams) kosher salt
1½ teaspoons (1.5 grams) orange zest
½ teaspoon (2 grams) almond extract
9¾ cups (1,220 grams) all-purpose flour, divided
1 cup (227 grams) unsalted butter, softened
⅓ cup (87 grams) Marzipan (recipe follows), frozen and grated
1 teaspoon (5 grams) whole milk
3 tablespoons (21 grams) sliced almonds

1. In a medium saucepan, bring amaretto and ¼ cup (60 grams) water to a boil over medium-high heat. Stir in raisins; remove from heat. Cover with plastic wrap, and let stand for 30 minutes. Strain, discarding excess liquid.
2. In the bowl of a stand mixer fitted with the paddle attachment, combine warm milk and yeast. Let stand until mixture is foamy, about 10 minutes. Stir in cream and orange juice.
3. With mixer on medium speed, add sugar, 2 eggs (100 grams), egg yolks, salt, zest, and almond extract, beating until combined. With mixer on low speed, gradually add 4½ cups (563 grams) flour, beating until combined. Add butter, 1 tablespoon (14 grams) at a time, beating until combined. Stir in raisins and Marzipan. Transfer dough to a large bowl, and stir in 4½ cups (563 grams) flour with a spatula or wooden spoon until combined. (Because this is such a large amount of dough, you will need to incorporate remaining flour into dough in a larger bowl.)
4. Transfer dough to a lightly floured surface, and knead until smooth and elastic, about 8 minutes, adding remaining ¾ cup (94 grams) flour, if needed. (Dough should not be sticky.)
5. Spray a large bowl with cooking spray. Place dough in bowl, turning to grease top. Loosely cover and let rise in a warm, draft-free place (75°F/24°C) until doubled in size, about 2 hours.
6. Preheat oven to 350°F (180°C). Line 2 baking sheets with parchment paper, and spray with cooking spray.
7. Lightly punch down dough. Cover and let stand for 5 minutes. On a lightly floured surface, turn out dough. Divide dough in half. Divide one half of dough into 4 equal pieces. Roll each piece into a rope about 15 inches long. Place strands vertically in front of you. Pinch 4 ends together at top. Cross the fourth strand over the second strand, the first strand over the third strand, and the second strand over the third strand. Repeat pattern until you've reached end of strands; pinch ends together to seal. Repeat with remaining dough. Place braided loaves on prepared pans. Cover and let stand in a warm, draft-free place (75°F/24°C) until puffed, about 30 minutes.
8. In a small bowl, whisk together milk and remaining 1 egg (50 grams). Brush dough with egg wash, and sprinkle with almonds.
9. Bake until golden brown and an instant-read thermometer inserted in center registers 190°F (88°C), 45 to 50 minutes, loosely covering with foil halfway through baking to prevent excess browning, if necessary.

MARZIPAN
Makes about 1 cup

1½ cups (144 grams) almond flour
1½ cups (180 grams) confectioners' sugar
1 large egg white (30 grams)
3 teaspoons (12 grams) almond extract
1 teaspoon (4 grams) rum extract

1. In the work bowl of a food processor, place flour and confectioners' sugar; pulse until combined. Add egg white and extracts; process until mixture holds together. If mixture is too dry, add water, 1 teaspoon (5 grams) at a time. Wrap tightly in plastic wrap, and refrigerate for up to 1 month.

WHITE CHOCOLATE-TAHINI BABKA

Tahini and babka hail from the same area of the globe, so it's only natural to marry them together in this sweet bread from cookbook author Ben Mims, perfect for breakfast or drenched in custard for a rich bread pudding. White chocolate doesn't compete with the tahini but offers a smooth sweetness to balance the flavor while orange zest delivers brightness to the heavy, sweet dough.

Makes 2 (9x5-inch) loaves

4¼ cups (531 grams) all-purpose flour
½ cup (110 grams) firmly packed dark brown sugar
3½ teaspoons (7 grams) instant yeast
1 teaspoon (3 grams) kosher salt
1 teaspoon (1 gram) orange zest
½ cup (112 grams) tahini
½ cup (120 grams) warm water (120°F/49°C to 130°F/54°C)
3 large eggs (150 grams)
¾ cup (170 grams) unsalted butter, softened
Ganache Filling (recipe follows)
9 ounces (250 grams) white chocolate, cut into ½-inch pieces
Brown Sugar Syrup (recipe follows)

1. In the bowl of a stand mixer fitted with the dough hook attachment, combine flour, brown sugar, yeast, salt, and zest.
2. In a small bowl, whisk together tahini, ½ cup (120 grams) warm water, and eggs until smooth. With mixer on low speed, add tahini mixture to flour mixture, beating until dough comes together. Add butter, 1 tablespoon (14 grams) at a time, letting each tablespoon incorporate before adding the next. Increase mixer speed to medium, and beat until smooth and elastic, about 10 minutes. Cover bowl with plastic wrap, and let rise in a warm, draft-free place (75°F/24°C) until doubled in size, 1½ to 2 hours.
3. Divide dough in half, and shape each half into a ball. Roll each ball into a 12x10-inch rectangle. Spread half of Ganache Filling onto each rectangle, leaving a ½-inch border on one short side. Sprinkle chocolate over Ganache Filling. Brush unfilled short side of each rectangle with water. Starting with opposite short side, roll up dough, jelly roll style, and press edges to seal. Place logs, seam side down, on a foil-lined baking sheet. Freeze for 15 minutes.
4. Spray 2 (9x5-inch) loaf pans with cooking spray. Line pans with parchment paper.
5. Transfer 1 log to a cutting board, and cut in half lengthwise. Place 2 halves cut side up, and carefully twist dough pieces around each other, leaving cut sides up. Nestle dough twist in one prepared

pan, tucking ends under, if necessary. Repeat with remaining log. Cover each loaf pan with a kitchen towel, and let stand at room temperature until dough rises to top of pans, 45 to 60 minutes.
6. Preheat oven to 350°F (180°C). Line a baking sheet with foil. Remove towels, and place loaf pans on prepared baking sheet.
7. Bake until deep golden brown on top and an instant-read thermometer inserted in center registers 190°F (88°C), 50 to 60 minutes, covering with foil to prevent excess browning after 20 minutes of baking, if necessary. Lightly drizzle warm Brown Sugar Syrup over each loaf. Let cool for 30 minutes to allow syrup to soak in completely. Remove from pans, and let cool completely on a wire rack.

GANACHE FILLING
Makes about 1½ cups

½ cup (120 grams) heavy whipping cream
⅓ cup (76 grams) unsalted butter
3 tablespoons (36 grams) granulated sugar
¼ teaspoon kosher salt
1 cup (170 grams) white chocolate morsels

1. In a small saucepan, bring cream, butter, sugar, and salt to a simmer over medium heat. Place white chocolate morsels in a medium heatproof bowl; pour hot cream mixture over morsels. Let stand for 1 minute. Slowly whisk chocolate mixture, starting in center and working your way to edges, until smooth. Refrigerate until chilled and spreadable, at least 2 hours.

BROWN SUGAR SYRUP
Makes ⅓ cup

⅓ cup (73 grams) firmly packed light brown sugar
⅓ cup (80 grams) water

1. In a small saucepan, bring brown sugar and ⅓ cup (80 grams) water to a boil over medium heat, stirring until sugar is dissolved. Reduce heat to low, and keep warm until ready to use.

Recipe by Ben Mims / Photo by Mason + Dixon

PANE DI PASQUA

This soft, slightly sweet bread with its iconic brightly colored eggs can be found well beyond the borders of Italy as a symbol of the Easter season.

Makes 1 (12-inch) wreath or 8 individual twists

3   cups (720 grams) boiling water
½   teaspoon (2.5 grams) liquid royal blue food coloring
1   tablespoon (15 grams) distilled white vinegar
5 to 8 large eggs (280 to 448 grams), in shell
Sweet Bread Dough (recipe follows)
1   teaspoon (5 grams) whole milk
1   large egg (50 grams), lightly beaten
Garnish: 1½ tablespoons (13.5 grams) sesame seeds, if desired

1. Place a wire rack on top of a sheet tray lined with paper towels.
2. In a medium bowl, whisk together 3 cups (720 grams) boiling water and food coloring. Stir in vinegar. Gently lower in-shell eggs (5 [280 grams] for wreath or 8 [448 grams] for individuals) into water mixture until desired color is reached, about 1 minute. Let dry completely on prepared rack, and refrigerate until ready to use.
3. Preheat oven to 350°F (180°C).
4. Lightly punch down Sweet Bread Dough. Cover and let stand for 5 minutes. On a lightly floured surface, turn out dough.
5. For wreath: Line a baking sheet with parchment paper, and spray with cooking spray.
6. Divide dough into 3 equal pieces. Roll each piece into a rope about 26 inches long. Place strands vertically in front of you. Pinch 3 ends together at top. Braid ropes together until you've reached end of strands. Join two ends together, forming a circle, and pinch ends to seal. Transfer to prepared pan. Gently tuck 5 dyed eggs between strands of dough. Cover and let stand in a warm, draft-free place (75°F/24°C) until puffed, about 30 minutes.
7. In a small bowl, whisk together milk and lightly beaten egg (50 grams). Brush dough with egg wash, avoiding dyed eggs.
8. Bake until golden brown and an instant-read thermometer inserted in center registers 190°F (88°C), 30 to 35 minutes, loosely covering with foil to prevent excess browning, if necessary.
9. For individuals: Line 2 baking sheets with parchment paper, and spray with cooking spray.

10. Divide dough into 8 equal pieces. Divide each piece in half. Roll each piece into a rope about 12 inches long. Place 2 strands vertically in front of you. Pinch ends together at top. Twist 2 pieces together until you've reached end of strands. Join two ends together, forming a circle, and pinch ends to seal. Transfer to prepared pans. Repeat with remaining dough. Place 1 dyed egg in center of each circle. Cover and let stand in a warm, draft-free place (75°F/24°C) until puffed, about 30 minutes.
11. In a small bowl, whisk together milk and remaining 1 egg (50 grams). Brush dough with egg wash, avoiding eggs. Sprinkle with sesame seeds, if desired.
12. Bake until golden brown and an instant-read thermometer inserted in center registers 190°F (88°C), 20 to 25 minutes.

SWEET BREAD DOUGH

Makes 1 (12-inch) wreath or 8 individual twists

1½   cups (360 grams) warm whole milk (105°F/41°C to 110°F/43°C)
4½   teaspoons (14 grams) active dry yeast
4   large eggs (200 grams), lightly beaten
⅔   cup (133 grams) granulated sugar
2   teaspoons (6 grams) kosher salt
8¾   cups (1,094 grams) all-purpose flour, divided
1   cup (227 grams) unsalted butter, softened

1. In the bowl of a stand mixer fitted with the paddle attachment, combine warm milk and yeast. Let stand until mixture is foamy, about 10 minutes.
2. With mixer on medium speed, add eggs, sugar, and salt, beating until combined. With mixer on low speed, add 4 cups (500 grams) flour, beating until combined. Add butter, 1 tablespoon (14 grams) at a time, beating until combined. Transfer dough to a large bowl, and stir in 4 cups (500 grams) flour with a spatula or wooden spoon until combined. (Because this is such a large amount of dough, you will need to incorporate remaining flour into dough in a larger bowl.)
3. Transfer dough to a lightly floured surface, and knead until smooth and elastic, about 8 minutes, adding remaining ¾ cup (94 grams) flour, if needed. (Dough should not be sticky.)
4. Spray a large bowl with cooking spray. Place dough in bowl, turning to grease top. Loosely cover and let rise in a warm, draft-free place (75°F/24°C) until doubled in size, about 1 hour.

PRO TIP

This bread is best eaten fresh, but to extend its shelf life, wrap in a breathable material, such as a cotton towel or brown paper bag, and store at room temperature for up to 2 days. After baking, leave dyed eggs out at room temperature for no longer than 2 hours before refrigerating or discarding.

CINNAMON TWIST

We gave one giant roll a showstopping twist. Using granulated sugar in place of brown sugar creates a crispier exterior while the tender interior has an elegant cinnamon swirl. Serve in slices or pull apart.

Makes 1 (9-inch) twist

Cinnamon Roll Dough (recipe on page 109)
⅔   cup (133 grams) granulated sugar
2½ teaspoons (5 grams) ground cinnamon
½   cup (113 grams) unsalted butter, softened
1   large egg (50 grams), lightly beaten
Garnish: cinnamon sugar

1. Spray a 9-inch round cake pan with cooking spray.
2. Lightly punch down Cinnamon Roll Dough. Cover and let stand for 5 minutes. Turn out dough onto a lightly floured surface, and roll into a 21x12-inch rectangle.
3. In a small bowl, combine granulated sugar and cinnamon. Spread butter onto dough, and sprinkle with sugar mixture, leaving a ½-inch border on one long side. Brush egg over side of dough without filling.
4. Starting with one long side, roll dough into a log, pinching seam to seal. Place log, seam side down, on a cutting board, and cut in half lengthwise, leaving 1½ inches at top. Carefully twist dough pieces around each other, and form into a circle. Place in prepared pan, cut sides up. Let rise in a warm, draft-free place (75°F/24°C) until dough has puffed, about 30 minutes.
5. Preheat oven to 350°F (180°C).
6. Bake until a wooden pick inserted in center comes out clean, 50 to 55 minutes, covering with foil halfway through baking to prevent excess browning. Let cool in pan for 20 minutes. Remove from pan. Garnish with cinnamon sugar, if desired.

APRICOT SWEET BUNS

Once a precious commodity traded on the Silk Road, jewel-hued dried apricots offer a chance to enjoy the delicately tart fruit after their notoriously short season has come and gone. We use dried apricots as the sweet golden filling of our almond-flecked sweet buns and top them off with a sticky drizzle of Brown Sugar Glaze.

Makes 12

1   cup (240 grams) warm whole milk (105°F/41°C to 110°F/43°C), divided
2¼   teaspoons (7 grams) active dry yeast
⅓   cup (67 grams) granulated sugar
⅓   cup (76 grams) unsalted butter, melted
¼   cup (60 grams) sour cream
1   large egg (50 grams)
1½   teaspoons (6 grams) almond extract
4   cups (500 grams) all-purpose flour, divided
1   teaspoon (3 grams) kosher salt
Apricot-Almond Filling (recipe follows)
Brown Sugar Glaze (recipe follows)

1. In a medium bowl, combine ¾ cup (180 grams) warm milk and yeast. Let stand until mixture is foamy, about 10 minutes.
2. In the bowl of a stand mixer fitted with the paddle attachment, stir together sugar, melted butter, sour cream, egg, almond extract, and remaining ¼ cup (60 grams) warm milk.
3. In a large bowl, whisk together 3⅔ cups (458 grams) flour and salt. Stir half of flour mixture into sugar mixture. With mixer on low speed, add yeast mixture, beating just until combined. Beat in remaining flour mixture. Switch to the dough hook attachment. Beat at medium speed until smooth and elastic, about 4 minutes. Add remaining ⅓ cup (42 grams) flour, if needed. (Dough should not be sticky.) Spray a large bowl with cooking spray. Place dough in bowl, turning to grease top. Loosely cover and let rise in a warm, draft-free place (75°F/24°C) until doubled in size, about 1 hour.
4. Line 2 rimmed baking sheets with parchment paper.
5. Lightly punch down dough. Cover and let stand for 5 minutes. Turn out dough onto a lightly floured surface, and roll into a 21x13-inch rectangle. Spread Apricot-Almond Filling onto dough. Fold dough in thirds, like a letter, creating a 13x7-inch rectangle. Roll dough into a 13x8-inch rectangle. Cut ½ inch off each short end of rectangle. Cut dough into 12 (1-inch) strips. Twist each strip, and tie in a knot, tucking ends under. Place on prepared pans. Cover and let rise in a warm, draft-free place (75°F/24°C) until puffed, about 30 minutes.

6. Preheat oven to 350°F (180°C).
7. Bake buns, one batch at a time, until golden brown and a wooden pick inserted in center comes out clean, 15 to 20 minutes, covering with foil halfway through baking to prevent excess browning. Brush buns with Brown Sugar Glaze. Let cool on pans for 10 minutes. Serve warm. Store in an airtight container at room temperature for up to 3 days.

APRICOT-ALMOND FILLING
Makes about 1½ cups

1   cup (128 grams) dried apricots
⅓   cup (67 grams) granulated sugar
1   tablespoon (14 grams) unsalted butter, cubed
¼   teaspoon ground cinnamon
½   cup (57 grams) sliced almonds

1. In a small saucepan, bring apricots and water to cover by 1 inch to a boil over high heat. Reduce heat to low; cook until apricots are softened, about 20 minutes. Drain apricots, reserving 2 tablespoons (30 grams) cooking liquid.
2. In the work bowl of a food processor, place warm apricots, reserved 2 tablespoons (30 grams) cooking liquid, sugar, butter, and cinnamon; pulse until mixture has the texture of jam. Stir in almonds; let cool completely. Refrigerate in an airtight container for up to 1 week.

BROWN SUGAR GLAZE
Makes about ½ cup

¼   cup (55 grams) firmly packed light brown sugar
¼   cup (60 grams) water
1   vanilla bean, split lengthwise, seeds scraped and reserved

1. In a small saucepan, bring brown sugar, ¼ cup (60 grams) water, and vanilla bean and reserved seeds to a boil over medium heat. Remove vanilla bean, and let cool completely. Refrigerate in an airtight container for up to 3 weeks.

SWISS HEFEKRANZ

For an update on this braided beauty, we turned the almond flavor up a few notches by rehydrating golden raisins and cherries in amaretto before mixing them in with the dough. We love the sour-sweetness the cherries bring. Sliced almonds and a final dusting of confectioners' sugar lend a subtle elegance to this wreath's look.

Makes 1 (12-inch) wreath

1	cup (240 grams) plus 1 teaspoon (5 grams) water, divided
¾	cup (96 grams) golden raisins
¾	cup (96 grams) dried cherries
½	cup (120 grams) plus 2 tablespoons (30 grams) amaretto, divided
1	tablespoon (15 grams) fresh lemon juice
6½	cups (813 grams) all-purpose flour, divided
1	cup (240 grams) warm water (115°F/46°C to 120°F/49°C)
½	cup (120 grams) warm whole milk (115°F/46°C to 120°F/49°C)
3	large eggs (150 grams), divided
¼	cup (50 grams) granulated sugar
1	tablespoon (6 grams) instant yeast
1	tablespoon (3 grams) lemon zest
2	teaspoons (6 grams) kosher salt
½	cup (113 grams) unsalted butter, softened and cubed
2	tablespoons (14 grams) sliced almonds

Garnish: confectioners' sugar

1. In a small saucepan, bring 1 cup (240 grams) water, raisins, cherries, ½ cup (120 grams) amaretto, and lemon juice to a boil over medium heat. Reduce heat, and simmer until liquid is reduced by three-fourths and fruit is plump, about 20 minutes. Drain, and let cool completely.

2. In the bowl of a stand mixer fitted with the dough hook attachment, stir together 3 cups (375 grams) flour, 1 cup (240 grams) warm water, warm milk, 2 eggs (100 grams), granulated sugar, yeast, and remaining 2 tablespoons (30 grams) amaretto. Let rest until slightly bubbly, 15 to 20 minutes.

3. With mixer on medium-low speed, add fruit mixture, zest, salt, and remaining 3½ cups (438 grams) flour, beating until combined. Add butter, a few pieces at a time, beating until combined. Increase mixer speed to medium, and beat until smooth and elastic, about 7 minutes. Spray a large bowl with cooking spray. Place dough in bowl, turning to grease top. Cover directly with plastic wrap, and let rise in a warm, draft-free place (75°F/24°C) until doubled in size, about 1 hour.

4. Line a large baking sheet with parchment paper.

5. On a lightly floured surface, divide dough into 3 equal pieces. Roll each piece into a 24-inch-long rope, and place on prepared pan. Pinch ropes together at one end to seal, and braid. Form into a circle, pinching ends to seal. Loosely cover with plastic wrap, and let stand in a warm, draft-free place (75°F/24°C) for 30 minutes.

6. Preheat oven to 350°F (180°C).

7. In a small bowl, whisk together remaining 1 egg (50 grams) and remaining 1 teaspoon (5 grams) water. Brush wreath with egg wash. Sprinkle with almonds.

8. Bake until golden brown and an instant-read thermometer inserted in center registers 190°F (88°C), about 40 minutes, covering with foil after 30 minutes of baking to prevent excess browning, if necessary. Let cool completely on a wire rack. Dust with confectioners' sugar, if desired. Store in an airtight container at room temperature for up to 4 days.

1. Roll each piece of dough into a 24-inch-long rope. Pinch ropes together at one end to seal. To braid, cross left strand over middle strand. Cross right strand over strand that is now in the middle.

2. Form into a circle, pinching ends to seal.

CHOCOLATE-FILLED BABKA

Babka is all about the rich twisted filling. Here, tight coils of semisweet chocolate bring a touch of cocoa decadence to the traditional formula.

Makes 2 (9x5-inch) loaves

6⅓   cups (792 grams) all-purpose flour
1¼   cups (250 grams) granulated sugar, divided
1   tablespoon (9 grams) active dry yeast
1   tablespoon (3 grams) orange zest
5   large eggs (250 grams), divided
¾   cup (180 grams) warm whole milk (105°F/41°C to 110°F/43°C)
1   teaspoon (4 grams) vanilla extract
1   cup (227 grams) unsalted butter, softened
1   tablespoon (9 grams) kosher salt
½   cup (120 grams) plus 1 tablespoon (15 grams) water, divided
Chocolate Filling (recipe follows)

1. In the bowl of a stand mixer fitted with the dough hook attachment, combine flour, ¾ cup (150 grams) sugar, yeast, and zest. With mixer on low speed, add 4 eggs (200 grams), warm milk, and vanilla, beating until mixture comes together, 2 to 3 minutes. (If mixture remains too dry and crumbly, add more milk, 1 tablespoon [15 grams] at a time.)
2. With mixer on medium speed, add butter, 1 tablespoon (14 grams) at a time, letting each piece incorporate before adding the next. Add salt, beating just until combined, about 3 minutes. Increase mixer speed to medium, and beat until a smooth and elastic dough forms and pulls away from sides of bowl. (If dough does not pull away from bowl, add more flour, 1 tablespoon [8 grams] at a time.)
3. Spray a large bowl with cooking spray. Place dough in bowl, turning to grease top. Cover and let rise in a warm, draft-free place (75°F/24°C) until doubled in size, 1½ to 2½ hours. After dough has risen, refrigerate for 30 minutes. Alternatively, the dough can be made 1 day in advance, and the entire rise may take place in the refrigerator overnight.
4. In a small bowl, whisk together 1 tablespoon (15 grams) water and remaining 1 egg (50 grams).
5. Spray 2 (9x5-inch) loaf pans with cooking spray, and line with parchment paper.
6. Divide dough in half. On a heavily floured surface, roll half of dough into a 16x12-inch rectangle. Brush edges of dough with egg wash. Spread with half of Chocolate Filling, leaving a 1-inch border on long sides of dough. Starting at one short side, roll up dough, jelly roll style, and press edge to seal. Using a sharp knife, cut roll in half lengthwise. Carefully twist dough pieces around each other, and place in prepared pan, cut sides up. Repeat procedure with remaining dough and remaining Chocolate Filling. Place prepared pans on a foil-lined rimmed baking sheet. Cover and let rise in a warm, draft-free place (75°F/24°C) until doubled in size, 1 to 1½ hours.
7. Preheat oven to 350°F (180°C).
8. Bake for 30 minutes. Cover with foil, and bake until an instant-read thermometer inserted in center registers 190°F (88°C), about 35 minutes more.
9. In a small saucepan, bring remaining ½ cup (100 grams) sugar and remaining ½ cup (120 grams) water to a boil over medium-high heat, stirring occasionally, until sugar is dissolved. Remove from heat, and let cool slightly. Pour simple syrup over warm loaves while still in pans. Let cool in pans for 5 minutes before transferring to a wire rack.

CHOCOLATE FILLING
Makes enough for 2 loaves

1   cup (170 grams) semisweet chocolate morsels
¾   cup (170 grams) unsalted butter
¾   cup (90 grams) confectioners' sugar
⅓   cup (25 grams) unsweetened cocoa powder
1   teaspoon (3 grams) kosher salt

1. In a medium saucepan, melt chocolate and butter over medium heat, stirring frequently to prevent scorching, until chocolate is melted and smooth. Remove from heat, and whisk in confectioners' sugar, cocoa, and salt. Let cool to room temperature before using.

Pistachios bring a subtle nuttiness, the perfect amount of crunch, and a vibrant green swirl to this rich loaf.

Makes 2 (9x5-inch) loaves

PISTACHIO-FILLED BABKA

6⅓	cups (792 grams) all-purpose flour	1	teaspoon (4 grams) vanilla extract
1¼	cups (250 grams) granulated sugar, divided	1	cup (227 grams) unsalted butter, softened
1	tablespoon (9 grams) active dry yeast	1	tablespoon (9 grams) kosher salt
1	tablespoon (3 grams) orange zest	½	cup (120 grams) plus 1 tablespoon (15 grams) water, divided
5	large eggs (250 grams), divided		Pistachio Filling (recipe follows)
¾	cup (180 grams) warm whole milk (105°F/41°C to 110°F/43°C)		

1. In the bowl of a stand mixer fitted with the dough hook attachment, combine flour, ¾ cup (150 grams) sugar, yeast, and zest. With mixer on low speed, add 4 eggs (200 grams), warm milk, and vanilla, beating until mixture comes together, 2 to 3 minutes. (If mixture remains too dry and crumbly, add more milk, 1 tablespoon [15 grams] at a time.)
2. With mixer on medium speed, add butter, 1 tablespoon (14 grams) at a time, letting each piece incorporate before adding the next. Add salt, beating just until combined, about 3 minutes. Increase mixer speed to medium, and beat until a smooth and elastic dough forms and pulls away from sides of bowl. (If dough does not pull away from bowl, add more flour, 1 tablespoon [8 grams] at a time.)
3. Spray a large bowl with cooking spray. Place dough in bowl, turning to grease top. Cover and let rise in a warm, draft-free place (75°F/24°C) until doubled in size, 1½ to 2½ hours. After dough has risen, refrigerate for 30 minutes. Alternatively, the dough can be made 1 day in advance, and the entire rise may take place in the refrigerator overnight.
4. In a small bowl, whisk together 1 tablespoon (15 grams) water and remaining 1 egg (50 grams).
5. Spray 2 (9x5-inch) loaf pans with cooking spray, and line with parchment paper.
6. Divide dough in half. On a heavily floured surface, roll half of dough into a 16x12-inch rectangle. Brush edges of dough with egg wash. Spread with half of Pistachio Filling, leaving a 1-inch border on long sides of dough. Starting at one short side, roll up dough, jelly roll style, and press edge to seal. Using a sharp knife, cut roll in half lengthwise. Carefully twist dough pieces around each other, and place in prepared pan, cut sides up. Repeat procedure with remaining dough and remaining Pistachio Filling. Place prepared pans on a foil-lined rimmed baking sheet. Cover and let rise in a warm, draft-free place (75°F/24°C) until doubled in size, 1 to 1½ hours.
7. Preheat oven to 350°F (180°C).
8. Bake for 30 minutes. Cover with foil, and bake until an instant-read thermometer inserted in center registers 190°F (88°C), about 35 minutes more.

9. In a small saucepan, bring remaining ½ cup (100 grams) sugar and remaining ½ cup (120 grams) water to a boil over medium-high heat, stirring occasionally, until sugar is dissolved. Remove from heat, and let cool slightly. Pour simple syrup over warm loaves while still in pans. Let cool in pans for 5 minutes before transferring to a wire rack.

PISTACHIO FILLING
Makes enough for 2 loaves

1	cup (227 grams) unsalted butter, softened
1	cup (200 grams) granulated sugar
4	large eggs (200 grams)
¼	cup plus 2 tablespoons (47 grams) all-purpose flour
¼	cup (24 grams) almond flour
1	teaspoon (3 grams) kosher salt
½	cup Pistachio Paste (recipe follows)
½	cup (57 grams) finely chopped pistachios

1. In the bowl of a stand mixer fitted with the paddle attachment, beat butter and sugar at medium speed until creamy, 3 to 4 minutes. Add eggs, one at a time, beating well after each addition. In a small bowl, whisk together flours and salt. With mixer on low speed, gradually add flour mixture to butter mixture, beating until combined. Add Pistachio Paste and pistachios, beating just until combined.

PISTACHIO PASTE
Makes about 1 cup

⅓	cup (67 grams) granulated sugar
¼	cup (60 grams) water
1	cup (142 grams) toasted pistachios
¼	cup (24 grams) almond flour
3	tablespoons (42 grams) vegetable oil

1. Line a rimmed baking sheet with parchment paper. In a small saucepan, heat sugar and ¼ cup (60 grams) water until a candy thermometer registers 240°F (116°C). In a small bowl, place pistachios. Pour hot syrup over pistachios, stirring to coat. Transfer pistachios to prepared pan, and let cool slightly, about 10 minutes.
2. In the work bowl of a food processor, combine pistachios and flour; process until finely ground, about 2 minutes. With processor running, add oil, 1 tablespoon (14 grams) at a time, until mixture forms a smooth, thick paste, 8 to 10 minutes.
3. Shape paste into a log, and wrap tightly in plastic wrap. Pistachio Paste will keep for 1 month in the refrigerator or 6 months in the freezer.

ONION TWIST BREAD

Sweet onions, roasted garlic, and cheese give this fluffy and light dough a savory twist. Serve it in place of traditional dinner rolls to amp up your bread basket.

Makes 6 to 8 servings

¼   cup (60 grams) warm water (105°F/41°C to 110°F/43°C)
2   teaspoons (6 grams) active dry yeast
4¼   cups (540 grams) bread flour
¼   cup (50 grams) granulated sugar
2   teaspoons (6 grams) kosher salt
½   cup (113 grams) unsalted butter, softened and divided
1   cup (240 grams) whole milk
1   large egg (50 grams)
1   head garlic (45 grams)
2   tablespoons (28 grams) olive oil
1   large yellow onion (400 grams), chopped
½   cup (50 grams) grated Parmesan cheese
2   tablespoons (4 grams) fresh thyme leaves

1. In a medium bowl, stir together ¼ cup (60 grams) warm water and yeast. Let stand until mixture is foamy, about 5 minutes.

2. In a large bowl, stir together flour, sugar, and salt. In the bowl of a stand mixer fitted with the paddle attachment, beat ¼ cup (56.5 grams) butter at medium speed until creamy, 2 to 3 minutes. Add yeast mixture and one-fourth of flour mixture, beating until smooth. Add another one-fourth of flour mixture, milk, and egg, beating until smooth. Add remaining flour mixture, and beat until smooth.

3. On a lightly floured surface, turn out dough, and knead 10 to 12 times. Spray a large bowl with cooking spray. Place dough in bowl, turning to grease top. Cover and let rise in a warm, draft-free place (75°F/24°C) until doubled in size, 1½ to 2 hours.

4. Preheat oven to 400°F (200°C). Cut ¼ inch off top of garlic, and wrap garlic in foil. Bake until soft, about 1 hour. Let cool completely. Press garlic head, and remove roasted garlic; set aside.

5. In a medium skillet, heat oil over medium heat. Add onion; cook, stirring occasionally, until onion is caramel in color, 20 to 25 minutes. Let cool completely.

6. In the work bowl of a food processor, place onion, roasted garlic paste, cheese, thyme, and remaining ¼ cup (56.5 grams) butter; process until mixture forms a smooth, thick paste, 2 to 3 minutes.

7. On a heavily floured surface, roll dough into a 14x10-inch rectangle. Spread onion filling onto dough, leaving a 1-inch border on long sides. Starting at one long side, roll up dough, jelly roll style, and press edge to seal. Using a sharp knife, cut roll in half lengthwise. Carefully twist dough pieces around each other, and form into a circle. Using a cake lifter, place dough in a greased 10-inch cast-iron skillet. Cover and let rise in a warm, draft-free place (75°F/24°C) until doubled in size, about 1 hour.

8. Preheat oven to 350°F (180°C).

9. Bake for 30 minutes. Cover with foil and bake until an instant-read thermometer inserted in center registers 190°F (88°C), about 40 minutes more. Serve warm.

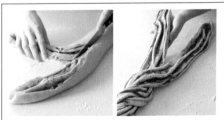

1. Using a serrated knife, cut roll in half lengthwise. With cut sides facing up, twist dough pieces around each other.

2. Form into a circle, pinching ends to seal.

NORWEGIAN JULEKAKE

In our babka-inspired take on Julekake, we replaced the raisins with rehydrated cranberries. Instead of mixing the cranberries in with the dough, we created a sweet jam-like filling flavored with cardamom and cinnamon. The Vanilla Glaze falls over every ridge and seeps into each crevice of this updated shape.

Makes 1 (12-inch) wreath

¾   cup (180 grams) whole milk
½   cup (100 grams) granulated sugar
¼   cup (57 grams) unsalted butter, softened and cubed
1½   teaspoons (4.5 grams) kosher salt
½   cup (120 grams) warm water (105°F/41°C to 110°F/43°C)
1   tablespoon (6 grams) instant yeast
2   large eggs (100 grams)
5½   cups (688 grams) all-purpose flour
1   teaspoon (2 grams) ground cardamom
Cranberry Filling (recipe follows)
Candied Lemon Peel (recipe follows), diced
Vanilla Glaze (recipe follows)

1. In a small saucepan, bring milk to a boil over medium heat. Remove from heat; add sugar, butter, and salt, stirring until completely incorporated. Set aside until cooled to 120°F (49°C) to 130°F (54°C).
2. In the bowl of a stand mixer fitted with the dough hook attachment, combine ½ cup (120 grams) warm water and yeast. Add warm milk mixture. Stir in eggs. With mixer on low speed, add flour and cardamom, beating until combined. Increase mixer speed to medium-low, and beat until smooth and elastic, 5 to 7 minutes. Spray a large bowl with cooking spray. Place dough in bowl, turning to grease top. Cover directly with plastic wrap, and let rise in a warm, draft-free place (75°F/24°C) until doubled in size, about 1 hour.
3. Line a large baking sheet with parchment paper.
4. On a lightly floured surface, roll dough into a 24x12-inch rectangle. Spread Cranberry Filling onto dough, leaving a ½-inch border on all sides. Sprinkle with diced Candied Lemon Peel. Starting at one long side, roll up dough, jelly roll style; press edge to seal. Place on prepared pan.
5. Using a serrated knife, cut roll in half lengthwise. With cut sides facing up, carefully twist dough pieces around each other. Form into a circle, pinching ends to seal. Loosely cover with plastic wrap, and let stand in a warm, draft-free place (75°F/24°C) for 30 minutes.
6. Preheat oven to 350°F (180°C).
7. Bake until golden brown and an instant-read thermometer inserted in center registers 190°F (88°C), about 40 minutes. Let cool completely on a wire rack. Drizzle with Vanilla Glaze. Store in an airtight container at room temperature for up to 4 days.

CRANBERRY FILLING
Makes about 1½ cups

1⅓   cups (171 grams) dried cranberries
⅓   cup (67 grams) granulated sugar
1   tablespoon (14 grams) unsalted butter, cubed
½   teaspoon (1 gram) ground cardamom
¼   teaspoon ground cinnamon

1. In a small saucepan, bring cranberries and water to cover by 1 inch to a boil over high heat. Reduce heat to low, and cook until cranberries are softened, about 20 minutes. Drain cranberries, reserving 2 tablespoons (30 grams) cooking liquid.
2. In the work bowl of a food processor, place warm cranberries, reserved 2 tablespoons (30 grams) cooking liquid, sugar, butter, cardamom, and cinnamon; pulse until mixture has the texture of jam. Let cool completely.

CANDIED LEMON PEEL
Makes about ½ cup

1   lemon (99 grams)
¾   cup (180 grams) water
1¼   cups (250 grams) granulated sugar, divided

1. Peel lemon, and slice peel into ¼-inch-thick strips.
2. In a small saucepan, bring peel and water to cover by 1 inch to a boil over medium heat. Boil for 15 minutes. Drain, and rinse with cold water.
3. In same pan, bring ¾ cup (180 grams) water and ¾ cup (150 grams) sugar to a boil over medium heat. Add peel. Reduce heat to medium-low, and simmer until peel is softened, 25 to 30 minutes. Drain.
4. Line a rimmed baking sheet with parchment paper.
5. Toss peel with remaining ½ cup (100 grams) sugar, and place on prepared pan. Let stand until dry, 1 to 2 days. Freeze in an airtight container for up to 2 months.

VANILLA GLAZE
Makes about ½ cup

1   cup (120 grams) confectioners' sugar, sifted
¼   cup (60 grams) heavy whipping cream
1   teaspoon (4 grams) vanilla extract
½   teaspoon (1.5 grams) kosher salt

1. In a small bowl, whisk together all ingredients until smooth. Use immediately.

STRAWBERRY COCONUT BABKA

Coconut flakes lend a delicate nuttiness to the sweet filling in this yeasted bread. We slather strawberry jam over the warm loaves post-bake.

Makes 2 (9x5-inch) loaves

¾ cup (180 grams) warm whole milk (105°F/41°C to 110°F/43°C)
1 tablespoon (9 grams) active dry yeast
5½ cups (688 grams) all-purpose flour
¾ cup (150 grams) granulated sugar
5 large eggs (250 grams), divided
1 teaspoon (4 grams) vanilla extract
1 cup (227 grams) unsalted butter, softened
1 tablespoon (9 grams) kosher salt
1 tablespoon (15 grams) water
Strawberry Coconut Filling (recipe follows)
¼ cup (80 grams) melted strawberry preserves, if desired
Confectioners' Sugar Glaze (recipe follows), if desired

1. Place milk in a small bowl. Gradually add yeast, whisking until completely dissolved. Let stand for 5 minutes.
2. In the bowl of a stand mixer fitted with the dough hook attachment, stir together flour and sugar until combined. With mixer on low speed, add yeast mixture, 4 eggs (200 grams), and vanilla, beating until mixture comes together, 2 to 3 minutes. (Mixture will be dry and crumbly.) Add butter, 1 tablespoon (14 grams) at a time, letting each piece incorporate before adding the next. Add salt, beating just until combined, about 3 minutes. Increase mixer speed to medium, and beat until a smooth and elastic dough forms and pulls away from sides of bowl.
3. Spray a large bowl with cooking spray. Place dough in bowl, turning to grease top. Cover with a double-layer of plastic wrap, and let rise in refrigerator overnight until almost doubled in size.
4. Line 2 (9x5-inch) loaf pans with parchment paper; spray with cooking spray. In a small bowl, lightly whisk together 1 tablespoon (15 grams) water and remaining 1 egg (50 grams).
5. Remove dough from refrigerator; divide dough in half. On a floured surface, roll each half of dough into a 16x12-inch rectangle. Spread half of Strawberry Coconut Filling onto each rectangle, leaving a 1-inch border on all sides. Brush edges of dough with egg wash. Starting at one short side, roll up dough, jelly roll style, and pinch edges to seal. Beginning 1 inch from one end, cut roll in half lengthwise using a serrated knife. Carefully turn each half cut side up; twist split portions around each other, pinching ends to seal. Transfer to prepared pans. Cover and let rise in a warm, draft-free place (75°F/24°C) until almost doubled in size, about 1 hour.

6. Preheat oven to 350°F (180°C).
7. Bake for 25 minutes. Cover with foil, and bake until an instant-read thermometer inserted in center registers 190° (88°F) to 200°F (92°C), 40 to 45 minutes more. Brush melted preserves onto warm loaves while still in pans, if desired. Let cool for 20 minutes. Remove from pans, and let cool completely on a wire rack. Drizzle with Confectioners' Sugar Glaze, if desired. Store in an airtight container at room temperature for up to 2 days.

STRAWBERRY COCONUT FILLING
Makes about 2 cups

3 tablespoons (24 grams) cornstarch
3 tablespoons (45 grams) fresh lemon juice
1½ cups (480 grams) strawberry preserves
1½ cups (98 grams) unsweetened flaked coconut

1. In a small saucepan, stir together cornstarch and lemon juice until smooth. Stir in preserves; bring to a boil over medium heat, stirring frequently. Reduce heat; simmer, stirring constantly, until thickened, 6 to 8 minutes. Transfer to a bowl; stir in coconut. Let cool completely.

CONFECTIONERS' SUGAR GLAZE
Makes about 1 cup

2 cups (240 grams) confectioners' sugar
3 tablespoons (45 grams) whole milk
⅛ teaspoon kosher salt

1. In a small bowl, stir together all ingredients until smooth. Use immediately.

Photo by Stephen DeVries

NUTELLA CRUNCH BRAID

This braided loaf is almost too pretty to eat. Almost. It combines the richness of chocolate and hazelnut with our basic dough for a treat that's perfect for breakfast or dessert.

Makes 1 (10-inch) braid

Basic Pull-Apart Bread Dough (recipe follows)
½ cup (128 grams) Nutella*
½ cup (57 grams) finely chopped skinned toasted hazelnuts

1. Spray a 10-inch round cake pan with cooking spray.
2. On a lightly floured surface, turn out Basic Pull-Apart Bread Dough. Punch dough down, and gently shape into a ball. Cover and let rest for 10 minutes.
3. Roll dough into a 16x14-inch rectangle. Spread Nutella onto dough, leaving a ½-inch border on all sides. Sprinkle with toasted hazelnuts. Starting with one long side, roll up dough, jelly roll style, and press edge to seal. Place dough, seam side down, on a cutting board. Using a serrated knife, cut roll in half lengthwise. Carefully twist dough pieces around each other, and form into a circle. Place in prepared pan, cut sides up. Cover and let rise in a warm, draft-free place (75°F/24°C) until doubled in size, about 45 minutes.
4. Preheat oven to 350°F (180°C).
5. Bake until golden brown and an instant-read thermometer inserted in center registers 190°F (88°C), 45 minutes to 1 hour, covering with foil halfway through baking to prevent excess browning, if necessary. Let cool in pan for 20 minutes before inverting onto a serving plate.

*We used Nutella, but any chocolate-hazelnut spread will work.

BASIC PULL-APART BREAD DOUGH

Makes 1 (10-inch) braid

⅔ cup (160 grams) warm whole milk (105°F/41°C to 110°F/43°C)
1 tablespoon (12 grams) granulated sugar
2¼ teaspoons (7 grams) active dry yeast
3¼ cups (406 grams) all-purpose flour, divided
¼ cup (57 grams) unsalted butter, melted
2 large eggs (100 grams)
1 teaspoon (3 grams) kosher salt

1. In the bowl of a stand mixer fitted with the paddle attachment, combine warm milk, sugar, and yeast. Let stand until mixture is foamy, about 10 minutes.
2. With mixer on low speed, add 1 cup (125 grams) flour, beating just until combined. Add melted butter and ½ cup (63 grams) flour, beating until combined. Beat in eggs.
3. Gradually add salt and remaining 1¾ cups (218 grams) flour, beating until a soft dough forms. (Dough will be sticky.)
4. Spray a large bowl with cooking spray. Place dough in bowl, turning to grease top. Loosely cover and let rise in a warm, draft-free place (75°F/24°C) until doubled in size, about 1 hour.

TRADITIONAL LARGE SOFT PRETZELS

From street fairs to football games, soft, doughy pretzels are everywhere. But you don't need a street vendor or concession stand to get your fix. With only seven ingredients in the dough and a short proof time, they're easy to make at home.

Makes 8

Pretzel Dough (recipe follows)
¼ cup (60 grams) baking soda
1 large egg (50 grams), lightly beaten
3 tablespoons (42 grams) unsalted butter, melted
Kosher salt or desired toppings (recipes on page 170)

1. Preheat oven to 400°F (200°C). Line 2 baking sheets with parchment paper, and spray with cooking spray.
2. Turn out Pretzel Dough, and divide into 8 equal pieces (about 5 ounces each). Starting from center and working outward, roll each piece into a log (2½ to 3 feet long and ¾ inch in diameter). Shape each log into a pretzel shape (see Pro Tip), and place on prepared pans. Cover and let rest for 5 to 10 minutes.
3. Bring a large pot of water to a boil over medium-high heat, and add baking soda. (Make sure pot is deep enough. Once you add baking soda, the water will expand an additional 2 inches.)
4. Drop each pretzel into boiling water-baking soda solution for 30 seconds per side. Remove from water using a large slotted spoon. Place back on prepared pans, and brush with egg wash.
5. Bake until golden brown, 10 to 13 minutes. Brush with melted butter, and sprinkle with salt or desired toppings.

PRETZEL DOUGH
Makes 8 large pretzels

1½ cups (360 grams) warm dark beer (120°F/49°C)
1 tablespoon (14 grams) firmly packed dark brown sugar
2 teaspoons (6 grams) active dry yeast
5 to 5½ cups (625 to 688 grams) all-purpose flour, divided
½ cup (120 grams) warm milk (105°F/41°C to 110°F/43°C)
2 tablespoons (16 grams) malt powder*
1 tablespoon (9 grams) kosher salt

1. In the bowl of a stand mixer fitted with the dough hook attachment, stir together warm beer, brown sugar, and yeast. Let stand until mixture is foamy, about 10 minutes.
2. With mixer on low speed, add 5 cups (625 grams) flour, warm milk, malt powder, and salt, beating until combined. Increase mixer speed to medium-high, and beat until dough is smooth and elastic, 5 to 6 minutes. Add remaining ½ cup (63 grams) flour, if needed. (Dough should not be sticky.)
3. Spray a large bowl with cooking spray. Place dough in bowl, turning to grease top. Cover and let rise in a warm, draft-free place (75°F/24°C) until doubled in size, about 1 hour.

Both diastatic and non-diastatic malt powder will work for this recipe.

PRO TIPS

To get this classic shape, roll the dough into a log, form elephant ears, then twist the ends together and wrap them underneath the bottom edge of the dough.

When boiling your pretzels, do 1 to 3 at a time, and pull out with a spider or slotted spoon so most of the water drains off before placing them on parchment paper to bake.

BREAKFAST BRAID

As they say, presentation is everything, and this braid delivers brunchtime wow. We wrapped some of our favorite breakfast foods like eggs (sunny-side up!), ham, and cheese in a homemade pizza dough.

Makes 1 (13-inch) braid

1½	cups (360 grams) warm water (105°F/41°C to 110°F/43°C)
4½	teaspoons (14 grams) active dry yeast
2½	teaspoons (10 grams) granulated sugar
4	cups (500 grams) all-purpose flour
2	teaspoons (6 grams) kosher salt
¼	cup (56 grams) olive oil
5	large eggs (250 grams), divided
1	pound (455 grams) thinly sliced smoked deli ham
1	(6-ounce) package (175 grams) sliced Swiss cheese
1	cup (55 grams) fresh baby spinach, stems removed
2	teaspoons (6 grams) black sesame seeds

1. In a small bowl, combine 1½ cups (360 grams) warm water, yeast, and sugar. Let stand until mixture is foamy, about 10 minutes.
2. In the work bowl of a food processor, place flour and salt; pulse until combined. With processor running, add yeast mixture and oil, pulsing until a ball forms. Transfer dough to a lightly floured surface, and knead until smooth.
3. Spray a large bowl with cooking spray. Place dough in bowl, turning to grease top. Loosely cover and let rise in a warm, draft-free place (75°F/24°C) until doubled in size, about 1 hour.
4. On a lightly floured surface, turn out dough. Punch dough down, and gently shape into a ball. Cover and let rest for 10 minutes.

5. Preheat oven to 400°F (200°C).
6. Spray a large skillet with cooking spray, and heat over medium-low heat. Gently crack 4 eggs (200 grams) into skillet; fry until yolks are set, 4 to 5 minutes.
7. On a sheet of parchment paper, roll dough into a 16x13-inch rectangle. Trim rough edges. Layer ham, cheese, and spinach lengthwise down center third of dough. Top with fried eggs. Using a pizza cutter or a sharp knife, cut ¾-inch diagonal strips on both sides of filling. Fold top and bottom pieces over filling, and braid strips of dough diagonally over filling, alternating left and right. Transfer to a baking sheet. Beat remaining 1 egg (50 grams), and lightly brush top of dough with egg wash. Sprinkle with sesame seeds.
8. Bake until golden brown, 20 to 25 minutes. Serve warm.

CHALLAH BRAID

Challah dough is enriched with eggs, oil, and yeast, with a little sugar for a hint of sweetness. We use honey in our version to achieve a slightly more complex flavor. The process is so easy and straightforward, you can turn out a from-scratch loaf in a short afternoon.

Makes 2 large braids

Challah Dough (recipe follows)
1 large egg (50 grams), lightly beaten
1 to 2 tablespoons (9 to 18 grams) poppy seeds

1. Line 2 baking sheets with parchment paper.
2. Divide Challah Dough in half. Divide one half into four equal pieces. Roll each piece into a rope about 18 inches long. Place strands vertically in front of you, and dust with flour. Pinch 4 ends together at top. Cross the first strand under the second and third strands. Cross the third strand over the second strand. Cross the fourth strand under the second strand. Cross the second strand over the third strand. Repeat this crossing pattern until you've reached end of strands; pinch ends together to seal. (See technique photos on pages 88-89.) Repeat with remaining dough. Place braided loaves on prepared pans. Loosely cover with plastic wrap, and let rise in a warm, draft-free place (75°F/24°C) until doubled in size, 45 minutes to 1 hour.
3. Preheat oven to 350°F (180°C).
4. Brush loaves with half of egg wash, and sprinkle with poppy seeds.
5. Bake until golden brown and an instant-read thermometer inserted in center registers 190°F (88°C), 35 to 50 minutes, brushing loaves with remaining egg wash halfway through baking, and covering with foil to prevent excess browning, if necessary. Let cool on pans for 10 minutes before serving.

CHALLAH DOUGH

Makes 2 large braids

1¾ cups (420 grams) warm water (105°F/41°C to 110°F/43°C)
2 tablespoons (24 grams) granulated sugar
1 tablespoon plus 1 teaspoon (12 grams) active dry yeast
½ cup (112 grams) olive oil
5 large eggs (250 grams)
½ cup (170 grams) honey
¼ cup (36 grams) kosher salt
8⅓ to 9 cups (1,042 to 1,125 grams) all-purpose flour

1. In the bowl of a stand mixer fitted with the dough hook attachment, combine 1¾ cups (420 grams) warm water, sugar, and yeast. Let stand until mixture is foamy, about 10 minutes.
2. With mixer on low speed, gradually add oil, beating until combined. Add eggs, one at a time, beating well after each addition. Beat in honey and salt. Gradually add flour, ½ cup (63 grams) at a time, beating until dough begins to pull away from sides of bowl. Increase mixer speed to medium-high, and beat for 3 to 5 minutes. (Dough will be sticky.)
3. Spray a large bowl with cooking spray. Place dough in bowl, turning to grease top. Cover and let rise in a warm, draft-free place (75°F/24°C) until doubled in size, 1 to 1½ hours.

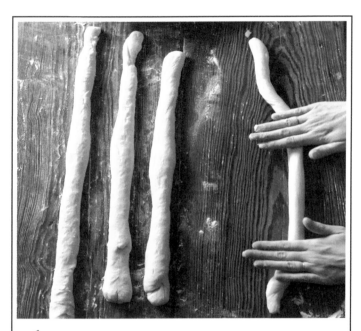

1 Divide one-half of dough into four equal pieces. Roll each piece into a rope about 18 inches long.

2 Place strands vertically in front of you, parallel to each other, and dust with flour. Pinch 4 ends together at top.

4 Cross the third strand over the second strand.

5 Cross the fourth strand under the second strand. Cross the second strand over the third strand.

CHALLAH BRAID
HOW-TO

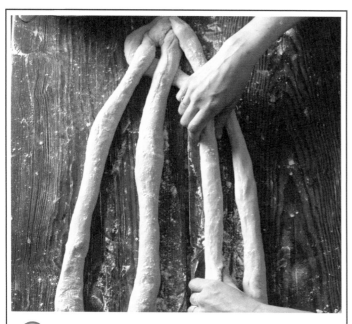

3 Cross the first strand under the second and third strands.

6 Repeat this crossing pattern until you've reached end of strands. Pinch ends together to seal.

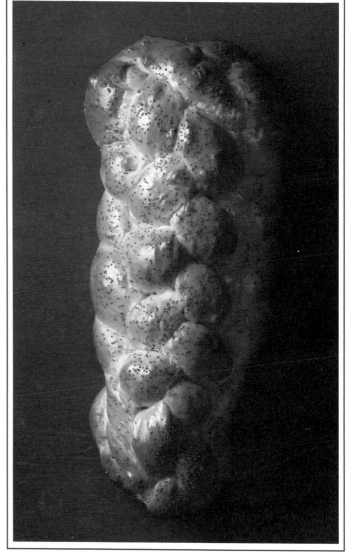

SMALL CHALLAH BUNS

Replace your go-to breakfast rolls with these individual buns, a challah twist on the traditional French raisin brioche, or pain aux raisins.

Makes about 10

½   recipe Challah Dough (recipe follows)
Vanilla Bean, Raisin, and Thyme Filling (recipe follows)
1   large egg (50 grams), lightly beaten

1. Line 2 baking sheets with parchment paper.
2. Divide Challah Dough into 10 equal pieces. Roll first piece into a 6x2½-inch rectangle. Sprinkle with Vanilla Bean, Raisin, and Thyme Filling. Starting at one long side, roll up dough, jelly roll style, and press edge to seal. Roll dough into a rope about 14 inches long. Cut rope in half crosswise; cut each piece in half lengthwise. Place the four strands in a hashtag pattern (over, under, over, under) with cut sides facing up. Take one piece, and cross it over an adjacent piece. Cross the next strand over an adjacent piece in the opposite direction. Repeat until all dough has been used. Tuck ends under, and place on prepared pans. (See technique photos on pages 92-93.) Repeat with remaining dough pieces and filling. Brush with egg wash. Loosely cover with plastic wrap, and let rise in a warm, draft-free place (75°F/24°C) until doubled in size, 30 minutes to 1 hour.
3. Preheat oven to 350°F (180°C).
4. Brush buns with egg wash.
5. Bake until golden brown, 15 to 25 minutes. Let cool on pans for 10 minutes before serving.

VANILLA BEAN, RAISIN, AND THYME FILLING
Makes about 1 cup

1   cup (128 grams) raisins
1   cup (240 grams) water
1   vanilla bean, split lengthwise, seeds scraped and reserved
10   sprigs fresh thyme

1. In a small saucepan, heat all ingredients over medium heat. Bring to a simmer; remove from heat. Cover and let stand for 20 minutes.
2. Discard thyme and vanilla bean pod; strain mixture to remove excess liquid. Let cool to room temperature before using.

CHALLAH DOUGH
Makes 20 small buns

1¾   cups (420 grams) warm water (105°F/41°C to 110°F/43°C)
2   tablespoons (24 grams) granulated sugar
1   tablespoon plus 1 teaspoon (12 grams) active dry yeast
½   cup (112 grams) olive oil
5   large eggs (250 grams)
½   cup (170 grams) honey
¼   cup (36 grams) kosher salt
8⅓ to 9 cups (1,042 to 1,125 grams) all-purpose flour

1. In the bowl of a stand mixer fitted with the dough hook attachment, combine 1¾ cups (420 grams) warm water, sugar, and yeast. Let stand until mixture is foamy, about 10 minutes.
2. With mixer on low speed, gradually add oil, beating until combined. Add eggs, one at a time, beating well after each addition. Beat in honey and salt. Gradually add flour, ½ cup (63 grams) at a time, beating until dough begins to pull away from sides of bowl. Increase mixer speed to medium-high, and beat for 3 to 5 minutes. (Dough will be sticky.)
3. Spray a large bowl with cooking spray. Place dough in bowl, turning to grease top. Cover and let rise in a warm, draft-free place (75°F/24°C) until doubled in size, 1 to 1½ hours.

PRO TIP
Make **Small Challah Buns with Chocolate-Hazelnut Orange Filling**. In step 2, spread chocolate-hazelnut spread onto dough, and sprinkle with orange zest.

Or don't use any filling, and simply sprinkle with poppy seeds after brushing with egg wash in step 4.

1 Divide dough into 10 equal pieces.

2 Roll first piece into a 6x2½-inch rectangle.

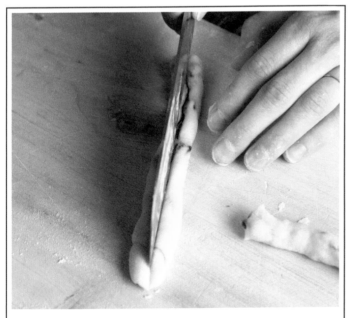

5 Cut rope in half crosswise; cut each piece in half lengthwise.

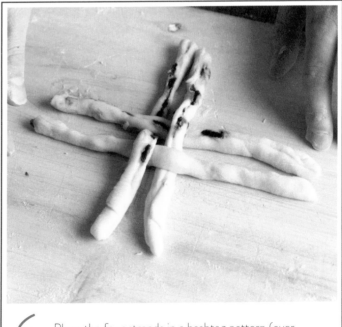

6 Place the four strands in a hashtag pattern (over, under, over, under) with cut sides facing up.

SMALL CHALLAH BUNS
HOW-TO

3 Sprinkle with Vanilla Bean, Raisin, and Thyme Filling. Starting at one long side, roll up dough, jelly roll style, and press edge to seal.

4 Roll dough into a rope about 14 inches long.

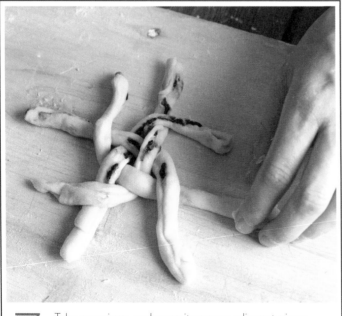

7 Take one piece, and cross it over an adjacent piece. Cross the next strand over an adjacent piece in the opposite direction. Repeat.

8 Tuck ends under, and place on baking sheets lined with parchment paper.

ROSEMARY FIG MARSALA ROUND CHALLAH

Once you've mastered the basic challah loaf, it's time to play around. We love the richness that the figs, vanilla bean, and Marsala add to this filled round.

Makes 1 round loaf

5   cups (640 grams) dried Turkish figs, stems removed
1   orange (131 grams), zested and juiced
1½   cups (360 grams) Marsala wine
6   sprigs fresh rosemary (23 grams)
1   vanilla bean, split lengthwise, seeds scraped and reserved
½   recipe Challah Dough (recipe follows)
1   large egg (50 grams), lightly beaten

1. In a medium saucepan, heat figs, orange zest and juice, Marsala, rosemary, and vanilla bean and reserved seeds over medium heat. Bring to a simmer, and reduce heat to low. Cook until figs are softened, about 10 minutes. Discard vanilla bean and rosemary; transfer mixture to the work bowl of a food processor. Process until mixture forms a thick paste. Let cool to room temperature before using.
2. Divide Challah Dough in half. Roll half of dough into an 18x12-inch rectangle. Spread half of cooled fig paste onto rectangle, leaving a ½-inch border on all sides. Starting at one long side, roll up dough, jelly roll style, and press edge to seal. Roll dough into a rope about 16 inches long. Cut rope in half lengthwise. Repeat with remaining dough and fig paste. You should have 4 (16-inch) ropes.
3. Line a baking sheet with parchment paper.
4. Place the four strands in a hashtag pattern (over, under, over, under) with cut sides facing up. Begin with any "under" strand, and moving clockwise, cross it over the adjacent strand. Repeat with the next strand until you get back to the beginning. Repeat this process moving counterclockwise. Continue repeating, clockwise and counterclockwise, until all dough has been used. (See technique photos on pages 96-97.) Tuck ends under, and place on prepared pan. Brush with egg wash. Loosely cover with plastic wrap, and let rise in a warm, draft-free place (75°F/24°C) until doubled in size, 30 minutes to 1 hour.
5. Preheat oven to 350°F (180°C).
6. Bake until golden brown and an instant-read thermometer inserted in center registers 190°F (88°C), 45 minutes to 1 hour, covering with foil halfway through baking to prevent excess browning, if necessary.

CHALLAH DOUGH

Makes 2 large round loaves

1¾   cups (420 grams) warm water (105°F/41°C to 110°F/43°C)
2   tablespoons (24 grams) granulated sugar
1   tablespoon plus 1 teaspoon (12 grams) active dry yeast
½   cup (112 grams) olive oil
5   large eggs (250 grams)
½   cup (170 grams) honey
¼   cup (36 grams) kosher salt
8⅓ to 9 cups (1,042 to 1,125 grams) all-purpose flour

1. In the bowl of a stand mixer fitted with the dough hook attachment, combine 1¾ cups (420 grams) warm water, sugar, and yeast. Let stand until mixture is foamy, about 10 minutes.
2. With mixer on low speed, gradually add oil, beating until combined. Add eggs, one at a time, beating well after each addition. Beat in honey and salt. Gradually add flour, ½ cup (63 grams) at a time, beating until dough begins to pull away from sides of bowl. Increase mixer speed to medium-high, and beat for 3 to 5 minutes. (Dough will be sticky.)
3. Spray a large bowl with cooking spray. Place dough in bowl, turning to grease top. Cover and let rise in a warm, draft-free place (75°F/24°C) until doubled in size, 1 to 1½ hours.

1 Divide dough in half. Roll one-half into an 18x12-inch rectangle.

2 Spread half of cooled fig paste onto rectangle, leaving a ½-inch border on all sides.

5 Place the four strands in a hashtag pattern (over, under, over, under) with cut sides facing up.

6 Begin with any "under" strand, and moving clockwise, cross it over the adjacent strand.

ROSEMARY FIG MARSALA ROUND CHALLAH HOW-TO

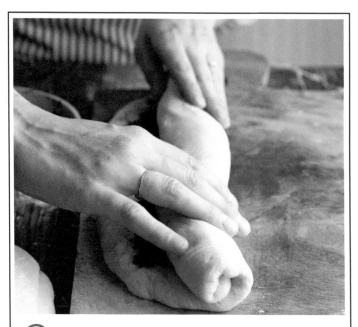

3 Starting at one long side, roll up dough, jelly roll style, and press edge to seal.

4 Roll dough into a rope about 16 inches long. Cut rope in half lengthwise. Repeat with remaining dough and fig paste. You should have 4 (16-inch) ropes.

7 Repeat with the next strand until you get back to the beginning. Repeat this process moving counterclockwise.

8 Continue repeating, alternating clockwise and counterclockwise, until all dough has been used. Tuck ends under, and place on prepared pan.

yeast BREADS

THE NATURAL LEAVENING POWER OF YEAST
CREATES FLUFFY PARKER HOUSE ROLLS, BILLOWY
BRIOCHE, AND A TOWERING PANETTONE

HONEY PEAR SWIRL BREAD

For this bread, we combined honey with pear preserves to create a silky filling that packs every bite with layers of fruit and spice.

Makes 2 (9x5-inch) loaves

2	cups (480 grams) warm whole milk (105°F/41°C to 110°F/43°C)
1	tablespoon plus 1 teaspoon (12 grams) active dry yeast
¾	cup (255 grams) honey, divided
2	large eggs (100 grams)
6	tablespoons (84 grams) unsalted butter, melted
1	tablespoon (9 grams) kosher salt
1	tablespoon (15 grams) fresh lemon juice
7½	cups (953 grams) bread flour, divided
1	(11.5-ounce) jar (325 grams) pear preserves
2	tablespoons (16 grams) cornstarch
2	teaspoons (4 grams) ground ginger
1	large egg white (30 grams), lightly beaten
¾	cup (60 grams) old-fashioned oats

1. In the bowl of a stand mixer fitted with the paddle attachment, combine warm milk and yeast. Let stand until mixture is foamy, about 5 minutes. Add ¼ cup (85 grams) honey, eggs, melted butter, salt, and lemon juice; beat at medium speed until combined. Gradually add 3 cups (381 grams) flour, beating until smooth. Gradually add 4 cups (508 grams) flour, beating until a soft dough forms. (If dough is too sticky, add remaining ½ cup [64 grams] flour.)

2. Turn out dough onto a heavily floured surface, and knead until smooth and elastic, 4 to 5 minutes, sprinkling work surface with more flour as needed. Spray a large bowl with cooking spray. Place dough in bowl, turning to grease top. Cover and let rise in a warm, draft-free place (75°F/24°C) until doubled in size, about 2 hours.

3. In a medium saucepan, bring pear preserves, cornstarch, ginger, and remaining ½ cup (170 grams) honey to a boil over medium heat. Cook for 1 minute, stirring constantly. Remove from heat, and let cool for 30 minutes.

4. Spray 2 (9x5-inch) loaf pans with cooking spray. Divide dough in half. On a lightly floured surface, roll each half into an 18x9-inch rectangle. Spread half of filling onto one rectangle, leaving a ½-inch border. Starting at one short side, roll up dough, jelly roll style, and press edge to seal. Place roll, seam side down, in prepared pan. Repeat with remaining dough and filling. Cover and let rise in a warm, draft-free place (75°F/24°C) until doubled in size, about 45 minutes.

5. Preheat oven to 350°F (190°C).

6. Brush top of loaves with egg white, and sprinkle with oats.

7. Bake for 45 to 50 minutes, covering with foil 30 minutes into baking to prevent excess browning, if necessary. Let cool on a wire rack.

CHESTNUT, CRANBERRY, AND ROSEMARY LAMINATED PAIN D'EPI

Fresh rosemary and fragrant chestnuts lend warm savory notes to the buttery bread studded with sweet cranberries.

Makes 2 loaves

3⅔ cups (466 grams) plus 1¼ cups (159 grams) bread flour, divided
1¾ cups (420 grams) plus 2 teaspoons (10 grams) warm water (105°F/41°C to 110°F/43°C), divided
2⅛ teaspoons (4 grams) instant yeast, divided
6 teaspoons (18 grams) kosher salt, divided
1 teaspoon (4 grams) granulated sugar
1¼ cups (183 grams) Roasted Chestnuts (recipe follows), chopped
¾ cup (96 grams) dried cranberries
¾ cup (170 grams) unsalted butter, softened
2 tablespoons (4 grams) chopped fresh rosemary
1 large egg (50 grams)
2 cups (480 grams) ice water
¼ cup (56 grams) olive oil

1. In a medium bowl, combine 1¼ cups (159 grams) flour, ½ cup (120 grams) warm water, and ⅛ teaspoon yeast. Cover with plastic wrap, and let stand at room temperature for 16 hours.
2. In the bowl of a stand mixer fitted with the dough hook attachment, beat yeast mixture, 1¼ cups (300 grams) warm water, 4 teaspoons (12 grams) salt, sugar, remaining 3⅔ cups (466 grams) flour, and remaining 2 teaspoons (4 grams) yeast at medium-low speed for 6 minutes. Increase mixer speed to medium, and beat for 2 minutes. Add Roasted Chestnuts and cranberries, beating just until combined, about 1 minute. Shape dough into a ball.
3. Spray a large bowl with cooking spray. Place dough in bowl, turning to grease top. Cover with plastic wrap, and let rise in a warm, draft-free place (75°F/24°C) until doubled in size, about 1 hour.
4. Between 2 sheets of plastic wrap, shape butter into a 10x8-inch rectangle. Sprinkle with rosemary, and wrap in plastic wrap. Refrigerate for at least 20 minutes or up to 24 hours. Let stand at room temperature for 10 minutes before using.
5. Preheat oven to 400°F (200°C). Position oven rack to lowest level, and place a large cast-iron skillet on rack. Line a baking sheet with parchment paper.
6. Freeze dough for 10 minutes. On a lightly floured surface, roll dough into a 16x10-inch rectangle. Unwrap butter block, and place in center of rectangle. Fold dough edges over to enclose butter block. Roll dough into a 24x8-inch rectangle. Fold one short side over 3 inches. Fold

other short side over 9 inches, making ends meet. Fold dough in half, creating an 8x6-inch rectangle. Roll into an 18x8-inch rectangle. Fold dough into thirds, like a letter, creating an 8x6-inch rectangle. Cover with plastic wrap, and let rest for 10 minutes.
7. Roll dough into a 19x11-inch rectangle. Trim ½ inch off all sides of dough. Cut dough in half lengthwise, creating 2 (18x5-inch) rectangles. Starting at one long side, roll up 1 rectangle, pinching seam to seal. Transfer to prepared pan. Repeat with remaining dough.
8. Using kitchen scissors, make a 45-degree cut into dough 1 inch from end, leaving about ¼ inch of dough uncut. (Be careful not to cut all the way through dough.) Lay dough piece over to one side. Make another 1-inch cut, and lay to other side. Repeat process until you reach end of dough. Repeat with remaining loaf.
9. In a small bowl, whisk together egg and remaining 2 teaspoons (10 grams) warm water. Brush egg wash onto dough. Pour 2 cups (480 grams) ice water in cast-iron skillet, and place loaves in hot oven.
10. Bake until deep golden brown, 25 to 30 minutes. Brush with oil, and sprinkle with remaining 2 teaspoons (6 grams) salt. Let cool slightly on a wire rack. Serve warm. Store in airtight container at room temperature for up to 4 days.

ROASTED CHESTNUTS
Makes about 4 cups

6 cups (892 grams) whole chestnuts in shells

1. Preheat oven to 425°F (220°C). Using a sharp paring knife, cut an "X" in rounded side of chestnuts. (This lets steam escape, and will prevent them from exploding.) Place on a rimmed baking sheet, cut side up.
2. Roast until shells curl away from nutmeats, 20 to 30 minutes.
3. Wrap hot chestnuts in a kitchen towel, and squeeze gently to further loosen shells. Let stand until cool enough to handle. Peel shells from nutmeats. Use immediately, or store in a resealable plastic bag at room temperature for up to 24 hours.

CLASSIC HOT CROSS BUNS

Soft and pillowy with just the right amount of sweetness and spice—one bite into this classic and it will be in heavy rotation at your house.

Makes 12

1⅔ cups (213 grams) raisins
¾ cup (180 grams) warm apple juice (180°F/82°C to 185°F/85°C)
Hot Cross Buns Dough (recipe follows)
1 large egg (50 grams)
1 tablespoon (15 grams) whole milk
1 cup (125 grams) all-purpose flour
6 tablespoons (90 grams) water
Golden Syrup (recipe follows)

1. In a large bowl, combine raisins and warm apple juice. Cover with plastic wrap, and let stand for 20 minutes. Strain, discarding excess liquid.
2. Prepare Hot Cross Buns Dough as directed through step 2. Stir in raisins, and continue as directed.
3. Spray a 13x9-inch rimmed baking sheet with cooking spray. Lightly punch down dough, and let rest for 5 minutes. On a lightly floured surface, turn out dough. Divide dough into 12 pieces, and roll each piece into a ball. Place on prepared pan. Cover and let stand in a warm, draft-free place (75°F/24°C) until puffed and rolls are touching, about 30 minutes.
4. Preheat oven to 375°F (190°C).
5. In a small bowl, whisk together egg and milk. Brush top of rolls with egg wash.
6. In a medium bowl, stir together flour and 6 tablespoons (90 grams) water, 2 tablespoons (30 grams) at a time, until a thick paste forms. Using a pastry bag fitted with a Wilton #10 piping tip, pipe paste over top of rolls to form a cross over each.
7. Bake until golden brown, 20 to 25 minutes. Brush warm rolls with Golden Syrup.

HOT CROSS BUNS DOUGH
Makes 12 buns

1¼ cups (300 grams) warm whole milk (105°F/41°C to 110°F/43°C)
½ cup (100 grams) granulated sugar, divided
4½ teaspoons (14 grams) active dry yeast

5⅔ cups (709 grams) all-purpose flour, divided
1 teaspoon (3 grams) kosher salt
1 teaspoon (2 grams) ground cinnamon
¼ teaspoon ground nutmeg
¼ teaspoon ground allspice
⅓ cup (76 grams) unsalted butter, melted
2 large eggs (100 grams)

1. In the bowl of a stand mixer fitted with the paddle attachment, combine warm milk, ¼ cup (50 grams) sugar, and yeast. Let stand until mixture is foamy, about 10 minutes.
2. In a large bowl, whisk together 5⅓ cups (667 grams) flour, salt, cinnamon, nutmeg, allspice, and remaining ¼ cup (50 grams) sugar.
3. With mixer on low speed, add half of flour mixture to yeast mixture, beating just until combined. Beat in melted butter and eggs. Gradually add remaining flour mixture, beating until a soft dough forms. Switch to the dough hook attachment. Beat at medium speed until smooth, about 4 minutes, adding remaining ⅓ cup (42 grams) flour, if needed. (Dough should not be sticky.)
4. Spray a large bowl with cooking spray. Place dough in bowl, turning to grease top. Loosely cover and let rise in a warm, draft-free place (75°F/24°C) until doubled in size, about 1 hour.

GOLDEN SYRUP
Makes 2 cups

2½ cups (500 grams) granulated sugar, divided
2 tablespoons (30 grams) room temperature water
1⅓ cups (320 grams) boiling water

1. In a medium saucepan, stir together ½ cup (100 grams) sugar and 2 tablespoons (30 grams) room temperature water. Cook over medium-high heat, without stirring, until deep amber colored. Remove from heat, and stir in 1⅓ cups (320 grams) boiling water and remaining 2 cups (400 grams) sugar. Return to medium-low heat, and simmer, without stirring, until thickened, 20 to 30 minutes. Let cool to room temperature.

Note: *This recipe makes enough syrup to use for multiple recipes. Cover and refrigerate for up to 6 months.*

HOW TO PIPE IT LIKE A PRO
It's time for the final touch. You want your flour paste to be stiff enough to be able to pipe in a clean line but still manageable. If the mixture is too hard to pipe, try adding a bit more water. When piping, try to keep your movements fluid to evenly pipe the lines.

Brushing the Golden Syrup (or any glaze) on the hot cross buns while still warm will help the glaze adhere and allow a small amount to be absorbed into the bread, further sweetening your rolls.

The syrup will further thicken as it cools. You want it to be the consistency of simple syrup while hot and honey-like once cooled. If it is too thick to brush on your rolls, just microwave in 3- to 4-second intervals.

ORANGE CURRANT HOT CROSS BUNS

If you love orange breakfast rolls, these tender buns are for you. Studded with tangy orange juice-soaked currants and slathered with a Honey-Orange Glaze, it's pure citrus delight.

Makes 1 (15-inch) round

2¼ cups (288 grams) dried currants
1¼ cups (300 grams) warm no-pulp orange juice (180°F/82°C to 185°F/85°C)
1½ cups (360 grams) warm whole milk (105°F/41°C to 110°F/43°C)
¾ cup (150 grams) granulated sugar, divided
6¾ teaspoons (21 grams) active dry yeast
10 cups (1,251 grams) all-purpose flour, divided
1½ teaspoons (4.5 grams) kosher salt
1½ teaspoons (3 grams) ground cinnamon
½ teaspoon (1 gram) ground nutmeg
½ teaspoon (1 gram) ground allspice
½ cup (113 grams) unsalted butter, melted
6 tablespoons (90 grams) freshly squeezed orange juice, strained
4 large eggs (200 grams), divided
1¾ teaspoons (1.75 grams) orange zest
1 tablespoon (15 grams) whole milk
3 tablespoons (45 grams) rose water
½ cup (120 grams) water
Honey-Orange Glaze (recipe follows)

1. In a large bowl, combine currants and warm orange juice. Cover with plastic wrap, and let stand for 20 minutes. Strain, discarding excess liquid.
2. In the bowl of a stand mixer fitted with the paddle attachment, combine warm milk, ¼ cup (50 grams) sugar, and yeast. Let stand until mixture is foamy, about 10 minutes.
3. In a large bowl, whisk together 8 cups (1,000 grams) flour, salt, cinnamon, nutmeg, allspice, and remaining ½ cup (100 grams) sugar.
4. With mixer on low speed, add half of flour mixture to yeast mixture, beating just until combined. Beat in melted butter, freshly squeezed orange juice, and 3 eggs (150 grams).
5. Transfer dough to a large bowl, and gradually add remaining flour mixture, stirring with a spatula or a wooden spoon until a soft dough forms. (Because this is such a large amount of dough, you will need to incorporate ingredients in a larger bowl.) Stir in drained currants and zest. Knead until smooth, about 8 minutes, adding up to ½ cup (63 grams) more flour, if needed. (Dough should not be sticky.)

6. Spray a large bowl with cooking spray. Place dough in bowl, turning to grease top. Loosely cover and let rise in a warm, draft-free place (75°F/24°C) until doubled in size, about 1½ hours.
7. Preheat oven to 375°F (190°C). Line a 15-inch round pizza pan or stone with parchment paper, and spray with cooking spray.
8. Lightly punch down dough, and let rest for 5 minutes. On a lightly floured surface, turn out dough. Divide dough into 18 pieces, and roll each piece into a ball. Arrange balls on prepared pan in a circular pattern, leaving little space between pieces. Cover and let stand in a warm, draft-free place (75°F/24°C) until puffed and rolls are touching, about 25 minutes. (Rolls will rise to edge of pizza stone but will not spill over during baking.)
9. In a small bowl, whisk together milk and remaining 1 egg (50 grams). Brush top of rolls with egg wash.
10. In a medium bowl, stir together rose water and remaining 1½ cups (188 grams) flour. Add ½ cup (120 grams) water, 2 tablespoons (30 grams) at a time, until a thick paste forms. Using a pastry bag fitted with a Wilton #10 tip, pipe paste over top of buns to form a cross pattern.
11. Bake until golden brown, about 25 minutes. Brush warm rolls with Honey-Orange Glaze.

HONEY-ORANGE GLAZE
Makes ½ cup

½ cup (170 grams) clover honey
¼ cup (60 grams) freshly squeezed orange juice, strained

1. In a small saucepan, bring honey and orange juice to a boil over medium-high heat. Reduce heat to medium-low, and cook, stirring constantly, until slightly thickened, about 2 minutes. Let cool completely.

CLASSIC CINNAMON ROLLS

The stickier, the better with this timeless treat. One of our favorite comfort foods, the recipe originated in Sweden, where they actually observe a Cinnamon Roll Day (Kanelbullens dag) on October 4, but we recommend celebrating these rolls every chance you get.

Makes 10 to 12

Cinnamon Roll Dough (recipe follows)
¾ cup (165 grams) firmly packed light brown sugar
1 tablespoon plus 1 teaspoon (8 grams) ground cinnamon
½ cup plus 3½ tablespoons (162 grams) unsalted butter, softened and divided
1 large egg (50 grams), lightly beaten
½ cup (112 grams) cream cheese, softened
1½ cups (180 grams) confectioners' sugar
1 tablespoon (15 grams) whole milk

1. Spray a 10-inch round cake pan or a 13x9-inch sheet pan with cooking spray.
2. Lightly punch down Cinnamon Roll Dough. Cover and let stand for 5 minutes. Turn out dough onto a lightly floured surface, and roll into an 18x12-inch rectangle.
3. In a small bowl, combine brown sugar and cinnamon. Spread ½ cup plus 2 tablespoons (141 grams) butter onto dough, and sprinkle with sugar mixture, leaving a ½-inch border on one long side. Brush egg over side of dough without filling.
4. Starting with one long side, roll dough into a log, pinching seam to seal. Trim ends. For round cake pan, slice into 10 rolls; for sheet pan, slice into 12 rolls. Place in prepared pan. Let rise in a warm, draft-free place (75°F/24°C) until puffed and rolls are touching, about 30 minutes.
5. Place a sheet of foil on bottom rack of oven, and preheat oven to 350°F (180°C).
6. Bake until a wooden pick inserted in center comes out clean, about 25 minutes. Let cool in pan for 10 minutes. Remove from pan.
7. In the bowl of a stand mixer fitted with the paddle attachment, beat cream cheese and remaining 1½ tablespoons (21 grams) butter at medium speed until creamy, 4 to 5 minutes. With mixer on low speed, gradually add confectioners' sugar, beating until fluffy. Stir in milk until combined. Spoon frosting onto warm rolls.

CINNAMON ROLL DOUGH
Makes dough for 10 to 12 rolls, 12 jumbo individual rolls, or 1 (9-inch) twist

If there were one go-with-the-flow dough, this would be it. Customize this adaptable dough to your personal preference. Simple yet forgiving, this one will become a staple in your recipe box.

1 cup (240 grams) warm whole milk (105°F/41°C to 110°F /43°C), divided
2¼ teaspoons (7 grams) active dry yeast
⅓ cup (76 grams) unsalted butter, melted
⅓ cup (67 grams) granulated sugar
¼ cup (60 grams) sour cream
1 large egg (50 grams)
4 cups (500 grams) all-purpose flour, divided
1 teaspoon (3 grams) kosher salt

1. In a medium bowl, combine ¾ cup (180 grams) warm milk and yeast. Let stand until mixture is foamy, about 10 minutes.
2. In the bowl of a stand mixer fitted with the paddle attachment, stir together melted butter, sugar, sour cream, egg, and remaining ¼ cup (60 grams) warm milk.
3. In a large bowl, whisk together 3⅔ cups (458 grams) flour and salt. Stir half of flour mixture into butter mixture. With mixer on low speed, add yeast mixture, beating just until combined. Beat in remaining flour mixture. Switch to the dough hook attachment. Beat at medium speed until smooth and elastic, about 4 minutes. Add remaining ⅓ cup (42 grams) flour, if needed. (Dough should not be sticky.)
4. Spray a large bowl with cooking spray. Place dough in bowl, turning to grease top. Loosely cover and let rise in a warm, draft-free place (75°F/24°C) until doubled in size, about 1 hour.

Photo by Stephen DeVries

PECAN CARAMEL CINNAMON ROLLS

The slight saltiness of the caramel drizzle and nuttiness of the pecans complement these sweet rolls perfectly for melt-in-your-mouth, ooey-gooey goodness. Toasting the pecans adds to their crunch and deepens their flavor.

Makes 12 jumbo rolls

Cinnamon Roll Dough (recipe on page 109)
½   cup (110 grams) firmly packed light brown sugar
1   tablespoon (6 grams) ground cinnamon
¾   cup (170 grams) unsalted butter, softened and divided
1   cup (113 grams) pecan halves, lightly toasted and chopped
1   large egg (50 grams), lightly beaten
1   cup (200 grams) granulated sugar
¼   cup (60 grams) water
⅓   cup (80 grams) heavy whipping cream
1   teaspoon (4 grams) vanilla extract
½   teaspoon (1.5 grams) kosher salt

1. Spray 2 (6-cup) jumbo muffin pans with cooking spray.
2. Lightly punch down Cinnamon Roll Dough. Cover and let stand for 5 minutes. Turn out dough onto a lightly floured surface, and roll into a 20x10½-inch rectangle.
3. In a small bowl, combine brown sugar and cinnamon. Spread ½ cup (113 grams) butter onto dough, and sprinkle with sugar mixture and pecans, leaving a ½-inch border on one long side. Brush egg over side of dough without filling.

4. Starting with one long side, roll dough into a log, pinching seam to seal. Trim ends, and slice into 12 rolls. Place in prepared muffin cups. Let rise in a warm, draft-free place (75°F/24°C) until dough has risen to just below rim of muffin cups, about 30 minutes.
5. Preheat oven to 350°F (180°C).
6. Bake until a wooden pick inserted in center comes out clean, about 25 minutes. Let cool in pans for 15 minutes. Remove from pans.
7. In a large saucepan, stir together granulated sugar and ¼ cup (60 grams) water. Cook over medium-high heat, without stirring, until mixture is amber colored. Remove from heat; stir in cream, vanilla, salt, and remaining ¼ cup (57 grams) butter. (Mixture will foam.) Let cool for 5 minutes. Drizzle over warm rolls.

KULICH

This tall, cylindrical Easter bread brims with the flavors of cardamom and apricots and the tang of sour cream, all topped with our lemon-tinged, made-from-scratch icing and garnished with multicolored sprinkles.

Makes 3

2¼   cups (540 grams) warm whole milk (105°F/41°C to 110°F/43°C)
4½   teaspoons (14 grams) active dry yeast
2¼   cups (450 grams) granulated sugar
9   large egg yolks (167 grams)
1   large egg (50 grams)
2   teaspoons (6 grams) kosher salt
1½   teaspoons (3 grams) ground cardamom
1½   teaspoons (9 grams) vanilla bean paste
12½ cups (1,563 grams) all-purpose flour, divided
2   cups (256 grams) dried apricots, finely chopped
1   cup (227 grams) unsalted butter, melted
¼   cup (60 grams) sour cream
Lemon Icing (recipe follows)
Garnish: multicolored nonpareil sprinkles

1. In the bowl of a stand mixer fitted with the paddle attachment, combine warm milk and yeast. Let stand until mixture is foamy, about 10 minutes.
2. With mixer on medium speed, add sugar, egg yolks, egg, salt, cardamom, and vanilla bean paste, beating until combined. With mixer on low speed, gradually add 6 cups (750 grams) flour, beating just until combined. Beat in apricots, melted butter, and sour cream.
3. Transfer dough to a large bowl, and stir in 6 cups (750 grams) flour with a spatula or wooden spoon until combined. (Because this is such a large amount of dough, you will need to incorporate remaining flour into dough in a larger bowl.)
4. Transfer dough to a lightly floured surface, and knead until smooth and elastic, about 8 minutes, adding remaining ½ cup (63 grams) flour, if needed. (Dough will be slightly soft and sticky but not unmanageable.)
5. Spray a large bowl with cooking spray. Place dough in bowl, turning to grease top. Loosely cover and let stand in a warm, draft-free place (75°F/24°C) until puffed, about 2 hours.
6. Preheat oven to 350°F (180°C). Spray 3 (5¼-inch) panettone molds with cooking spray.

7. On a lightly floured surface, turn out dough. Divide dough into 3 equal pieces. Shape each piece into a ball by folding the corners of the dough into the center. Place dough, seam side down, in prepared molds. Cover and let stand in a warm, draft-free place (75°F/24°C) until slightly puffed, about 30 minutes. (Remaining rising will happen as it gradually bakes.)
8. Bake, covered, until a wooden pick inserted in center comes out clean and an instant-read thermometer inserted in center registers 190°F (88°C), 1 hour to 1 hour and 10 minutes. Let cool completely. Spoon Lemon Icing over cooled Kulichs. Garnish with sprinkles, if desired.

LEMON ICING
Makes 1⅔ cups

4   cups (480 grams) confectioners' sugar
1   teaspoon (5 grams) fresh lemon juice, strained
½   cup (120 grams) whole milk

1. In a large bowl, whisk together confectioners' sugar and lemon juice. Stir in milk, 2 tablespoons (30 grams) at a time, until desired consistency is reached.

PRO TIP
Wrap in a paper bag or loosely wrap in foil, and store at room temperature for up to 2 days. Freezing bread is the best way to keep homemade bread fresh for longer. Wrap cooled bread tightly in plastic wrap, and freeze for up to 2 months.

COCONUT BUNS

These buns from cookbook author Ben Mims are the best breakfast treat around. Enriched with coconut milk and oil in the dough and filled with a sweetened, toasted coconut butter, this recipe is for the serious coconut lover. Make the dough and assemble buns the night before you plan to bake them for breakfast. Their flavor deepens with a long, slow rise in the refrigerator, but if you don't have the spare hours to wait, you can let them rise at room temperature for an hour and a half.

Makes 12

1¼	cups (300 grams) warm unsweetened canned coconut milk (120°F/49°C to 130°F/54°C)
⅓	cup (67 grams) granulated sugar
2	tablespoons (28 grams) unrefined coconut oil, melted
1	teaspoon (3 grams) kosher salt
1	large egg (50 grams), lightly beaten
4	cups (500 grams) all-purpose flour
3½	teaspoons (7 grams) instant yeast
½	cup (42 grams) unsweetened flaked coconut

Coconut Filling (recipe follows)
Coconut Icing (recipe follows)

1. In the bowl of a stand mixer fitted with the dough hook attachment, combine warm coconut milk, sugar, melted coconut oil, salt, and egg. Add flour and yeast, and beat at low speed until a dough forms. Increase mixer speed to medium, and beat until smooth, about 8 minutes. Cover with plastic wrap, and let rise in a warm, draft-free place (75°F/24°C) until doubled in size, about 1½ hours.

2. Preheat oven to 350°F (180°C). Spread coconut on a baking sheet, and bake, stirring halfway through, until lightly golden brown, about 8 minutes. Transfer coconut to a bowl, and let cool completely. Lightly grease a 13x9-inch baking pan with butter.

3. Transfer dough to a lightly floured surface. Roll into an 18x12-inch rectangle. Spread Coconut Filling onto dough, leaving a ½-inch border on one long side. Starting with opposite long side, roll dough into a tight log. Trim ends, and cut into 12 rounds. Place cut side up in prepared pan. Cover with plastic wrap, and refrigerate for at least 8 hours or overnight. (Alternatively, let rolls rise at room temperature for 1½ hours.)

4. Preheat oven to 375°F (190°C).

5. Bake until puffed and golden brown throughout, about 35 minutes. Let cool for 10 minutes. Drizzle Coconut Icing over warm rolls, and sprinkle with toasted coconut.

COCONUT FILLING

Makes 4 cups

1	cup (84 grams) finely shredded dried (desiccated) coconut
1	cup (227 grams) unsalted butter, softened
½	cup (110 grams) firmly packed light brown sugar
3	cups (360 grams) confectioners' sugar, sifted
1	teaspoon (4 grams) coconut extract
1	teaspoon (4 grams) vanilla extract
½	teaspoon (1.5 grams) kosher salt

1. Preheat oven to 350°F (180°C). Spread coconut on a baking sheet, and bake, stirring halfway through, until lightly golden brown, about 8 minutes. Transfer to a bowl, and let cool completely.

2. In the bowl of a stand mixer fitted with the paddle attachment, beat butter and brown sugar at medium speed until smooth, about 2 minutes. Add confectioners' sugar, extracts, and salt; beat until smooth. Reserve ½ cup filling for Coconut Icing. Stir toasted coconut into remaining filling. Cover with plastic wrap until ready to use.

COCONUT ICING

Makes ½ cup

½	cup Coconut Filling (recipe precedes)
2	tablespoons (30 grams) unsweetened canned coconut milk

1. In a small bowl, stir together Coconut Filling and coconut milk. Cover with plastic wrap until ready to use.

Recipe by Ben Mims / Photo by Mason + Dixon

[yeast breads]

PICKLED CHERRY BOMBS

These little pockets of dough pack explosive flavor. Inspired by Milk Bar founder Christina Tosi's famous Bagel Bomb creation, each savory orb offers all the chew and salty, crusty goodness of a regular bagel, but with an epic epicenter: a sour pickled cherry thickly coated in rich mascarpone, cream cheese, and fried garlic.

Makes 16

4   cups (508 grams) bread flour
1½   cups (360 grams) warm water (105°F/41°C to 110°F/43°C)
1   tablespoon (6 grams) instant yeast
1   tablespoon (21 grams) molasses
2   teaspoons (6 grams) kosher salt
8   cups (1,920 grams) plus 1 teaspoon (5 grams) water, divided
¼   cup (60 grams) baking soda
2   tablespoons (42 grams) honey
1   tablespoon (12 grams) granulated sugar
Pickled Cherry Cheese Balls (recipe follows)
1½   teaspoons (4.5 grams) sesame seeds
1½   teaspoons (4.5 grams) poppy seeds
1   teaspoon (3 grams) fennel seeds
1   teaspoon (2 grams) garlic salt
1   teaspoon (2 grams) diced onion flakes
½   teaspoon (1.5 gram) sea salt
1   large egg (50 grams)

1. In the bowl of a stand mixer fitted with the dough hook attachment, beat flour, 1½ cups (360 grams) warm water, yeast, molasses, and kosher salt at medium-low speed for 10 minutes. Spray a large bowl with cooking spray. Place dough in bowl, turning to grease top. Cover with plastic wrap, and let rise in warm, draft-free place (75°F/24°C) until almost doubled in size, 1 to 1½ hours.
2. Divide dough into 16 (2-ounce) pieces, and shape into balls. Loosely cover with plastic wrap, and let rest for 30 minutes.
3. Preheat oven to 350°F (180°C). Line 2 baking sheets with parchment paper.
4. In a large stockpot, bring 8 cups (1,920 grams) water, baking soda, honey, and sugar to a boil over medium-high heat. Pull and shape dough balls into 3½-inch disks, like pizzas. Place a frozen Pickled Cherry Cheese Ball in center of each disk; bring edges up, and pinch together. Roll dough between hands to smooth out ball

and ensure edges are sealed. Working with 4 balls at a time, lower balls into poaching liquid. Boil for 1 minute, turning halfway through. Transfer to prepared pans.
5. In a small bowl, whisk together sesame seeds, poppy seeds, fennel seeds, garlic salt, onion flakes, and sea salt. In another small bowl, whisk together egg and remaining 1 teaspoon (5 grams) water. Brush top of each ball with egg wash, and sprinkle with topping.
6. Bake until light golden, 20 to 25 minutes. Let cool slightly; serve warm.

PICKLED CHERRY CHEESE BALLS
Makes 16

1   tablespoon (14 grams) olive oil
1   tablespoon (10 grams) minced garlic
½   cup (112 grams) cream cheese, softened
½   cup (112 grams) mascarpone cheese, softened
½   teaspoon chopped fresh basil
½   teaspoon chopped fresh oregano
½   teaspoon chopped fresh thyme
½   teaspoon (1.5 grams) kosher salt
16   Pickled Cherries (recipe follows)

1. In a small saucepan, heat oil over medium heat. Add garlic; cook until golden, 2 to 3 minutes. Remove from heat, and let cool completely.
2. In the bowl of a stand mixer fitted with the paddle attachment, beat garlic, cream cheese, mascarpone, basil, oregano, thyme, and salt at medium speed until combined.
3. Pat Pickled Cherries dry with a paper towel. Working with one at a time, coat Pickled Cherries with cheese mixture, rolling between hands to create well-rounded balls. Freeze in an airtight container for at least 2 hours or up to 1 week.

PICKLED CHERRIES
Makes 1 quart

½   pound (225 grams) cherries, pitted
¾   cup (180 grams) distilled white vinegar
⅓   cup (67 grams) granulated sugar
½   tablespoon (4.5 grams) kosher salt
1   strip orange zest
1   cinnamon stick
½   teaspoon (1.5 gram) black peppercorns
½   teaspoon (1 gram) crushed red pepper

1. Place cherries in a 1-quart jar.
2. In a small saucepan, bring vinegar and all remaining ingredients to a boil over medium heat. Reduce heat to medium-low, and simmer for 10 minutes. Remove from heat, and let cool for 10 minutes.
3. Strain mixture through a fine-mesh sieve over cherries, discarding solids. Cherries should be completely submerged under liquid. If not completely submerged, top off with more vinegar. Let cool completely. Cover and refrigerate for at least 30 minutes or up to 1 month.

CHERRY SWEET ROLLS

Give your go-to cinnamon rolls a break. These fluffy sweet rolls taste like the breakfast version of cherry pie.

Makes 12

¼ cup (60 grams) warm water (105°F/41°C to 110°F/43°C)
2 teaspoons (6 grams) active dry yeast
½ cup (100 grams) plus 2⅓ tablespoons (28 grams) granulated sugar, divided
½ cup (113 grams) unsalted butter, softened
2 teaspoons (6 grams) kosher salt
1¼ cups (300 grams) whole milk, divided
2 large eggs (100 grams)
1 tablespoon (15 grams) fresh lemon juice
5¼ cups (667 grams) bread flour
1 (12-ounce) bag (340 grams) frozen dark sweet cherries, thawed, juice drained and reserved
1 tablespoon (8 grams) cornstarch
⅓ cup (107 grams) cherry preserves
2½ cups (300 grams) confectioners' sugar, divided
2 tablespoons (28 grams) unsalted butter, melted
½ teaspoon (2 grams) vanilla extract

1. In a small bowl, stir together ¼ cup (60 grams) water, yeast, and 1 teaspoon (4 grams) granulated sugar. Let stand until mixture is foamy, about 5 minutes.

2. In the bowl of a stand mixer fitted with the paddle attachment, beat butter at medium speed until creamy, 2 to 3 minutes. Gradually add ½ cup (100 grams) granulated sugar and salt, beating until creamy, 3 to 4 minutes, stopping to scrape sides of bowl. Add 1 cup (240 grams) milk, eggs, and lemon juice, beating until combined. Stir in yeast mixture. With mixer on low speed, gradually add flour, beating until well combined, about 2 minutes.

3. On a lightly floured surface, turn out dough, and knead for 5 minutes. Spray a large bowl with cooking spray. Place dough in bowl, turning to grease top. Cover and let rise in a warm, draft-free place (75°F/24°C) until doubled in size, about 1½ hours.

4. In a medium saucepan, combine cherries, cornstarch, and remaining 2 tablespoons (24 grams) granulated sugar. Cook over medium heat, stirring constantly, until bubbly and thickened, 3 to 4 minutes. Remove from heat, and stir in preserves. Let cool completely.

5. Spray 2 (9-inch) cast-iron skillets with cooking spray.

6. Lightly punch down dough. On a lightly floured surface, roll dough into an 18x10-inch rectangle. Spread cherry mixture onto dough. Starting at one long side, roll up dough, jelly roll style, and press edge to seal. Slice into 12 rolls, and place in prepared pans. Cover and let rise in a warm, draft-free place (75°F/24°C) until doubled in size, about 45 minutes.

7. Preheat oven to 350°F (180°C).

8. Bake until golden brown, 25 to 30 minutes. Let cool in pans for 5 minutes.

9. In a small bowl, whisk together 1 cup (120 grams) confectioners' sugar, 3 tablespoons (45 grams) reserved cherry juice, and melted butter. Brush onto hot rolls. Let cool for 30 minutes.

10. In a medium bowl, whisk together vanilla, remaining 1½ cups (180 grams) confectioners' sugar, and remaining ¼ cup (60 grams) milk until smooth; drizzle over rolls.

SWEET POTATO BISCUITS

With a hint of aromatic sage and a generous coating of Honey Butter, these tender biscuits will warm your soul with every bite.

Makes 9

2¼   cups (281 grams) all-purpose flour
1   tablespoon (15 grams) baking powder
2   teaspoons (6 grams) kosher salt
1   teaspoon (2 grams) instant yeast
½   teaspoon (2.5 grams) baking soda
6   tablespoons (84 grams) cold unsalted butter, cubed
¼   cup (8 grams) chopped fresh sage
½   cup (120 grams) cold whole buttermilk
¼   cup (85 grams) golden honey
1   cup (244 grams) mashed sweet potato, chilled
¼   cup (57 grams) unsalted butter, melted
Honey Butter (see Pro Tip)

1. Preheat oven to 425°F (220°C). Line a baking sheet with parchment paper.
2. In a large bowl, whisk together flour, baking powder, salt, yeast, and baking soda. Using a pastry blender, cut in cold butter until mixture is crumbly. Stir in sage. In a small bowl, whisk together buttermilk and honey; quickly stir buttermilk mixture into flour mixture until combined. (Do not overmix.) Stir in sweet potato.
3. Turn out dough onto a lightly floured surface, and knead very gently 5 or 6 times until dough comes together but is still slightly lumpy. (If dough is too sticky, work in up to ¼ cup [31 grams] more flour.) Shape dough into a disk, and pat to 1-inch thickness. Using a 2-inch round cutter dipped in flour, cut dough, rerolling scraps as necessary. Place biscuits on prepared pan. Brush with melted butter.
4. Bake until golden brown, 12 to 15 minutes, rotating pan halfway through baking. Serve with Honey Butter.

PRO TIP
To make **Honey Butter,** in a medium bowl, stir together ½ cup (113 grams) softened unsalted butter and ¼ cup (85 grams) honey until combined. Cover and refrigerate for up to 1 week.

BISCUIT STIR-INS

Ginger and Thyme: Substitute chopped fresh sage with 3 tablespoons (32 grams) chopped candied ginger and 1 tablespoon (2 grams) fresh thyme leaves. Proceed as directed.

Rosemary and Parmesan: Substitute chopped fresh sage with 1 tablespoon (2 grams) chopped fresh rosemary and ¼ cup (25 grams) freshly grated Parmesan cheese.

Orange and Rosemary: Substitute chopped fresh sage with 1 tablespoon (3 grams) orange zest and 1 tablespoon (2 grams) chopped fresh rosemary.

LAMINATED BISCUITS

This is our biscuit-croissant hybrid—our criscuit, if you will. They are delicately layered and especially flaky. Splurge on the highest-quality butter you can find to get the best results with these.

Makes about 18

¼   cup (50 grams) granulated sugar
3   tablespoons (45 grams) warm water (105°F/41°C to 110°F/43°C)
2   teaspoons (6 grams) active dry yeast
5   cups (625 grams) plus 2 tablespoons (16 grams) all-purpose flour, divided
3   teaspoons (9 grams) kosher salt, divided
1   teaspoon (5 grams) baking soda
1   teaspoon (5 grams) baking powder
½   cup (113 grams) all-vegetable shortening, cubed
½   cup (113 grams) cold unsalted butter, cubed
2   cups (480 grams) whole buttermilk
1   cup (227 grams) unsalted butter, softened
¼   cup (57 grams) unsalted butter, melted

1. In a small bowl, stir together sugar, 3 tablespoons (45 grams) warm water, and yeast. Let stand until mixture is foamy, about 5 minutes.

2. In a medium bowl, whisk together 5 cups (625 grams) flour, 2 teaspoons (6 grams) salt, baking soda, and baking powder. Using your fingers, cut in shortening and cold butter until mixture is crumbly. Add yeast mixture and buttermilk, stirring just until dry ingredients are moistened. Knead by hand 2 to 3 times until dough comes together. Spray a large bowl with cooking spray. Place dough in bowl, turning to grease top. Cover and let rise in a warm, draft-free place (75°F/24°C) until puffed, 1½ to 2 hours.

3. In the bowl of a stand mixer fitted with the paddle attachment, beat softened butter, remaining 2 tablespoons (16 grams) flour, and remaining 1 teaspoon (3 grams) salt at medium speed until creamy and well combined, 3 to 4 minutes. On a sheet of plastic wrap, spread beaten butter mixture into a 10x8-inch rectangle. Wrap in plastic wrap, and refrigerate until firm, at least 30 minutes.

4. Preheat oven to 400°F (200°C). Line 2 baking sheets with parchment paper.

5. Turn out dough onto a lightly floured surface. Gently pat dough into an 18x12-inch rectangle. Unwrap butter block, and place in center of dough. Fold dough into thirds, like a letter. Pat dough to 1½-inch thickness. Rotate dough 90 degrees, and fold dough again into thirds, like a letter. Pat dough to 1-inch thickness. Using a 2½-inch round cutter, cut dough, re-patting scraps as necessary. Place on prepared pan. Brush with melted butter.

6. Bake until golden brown, 15 to 20 minutes. Let cool on pan for 5 minutes. Serve warm.

1

Snap butter with your fingertips to break it up and mix into flour to get the best consistency for biscuit dough. A food processor will work if you are in a hurry, but it is best to use your fingers. The small pieces of butter aerate the dough to make the biscuits rise. Before snapping, make sure your hands are cold. If necessary, dunk warm hands in ice water and dry them before immersing into the butter and flour mixture.

Try to incorporate butter into the dry ingredients as fast as possible, and start turning the mixture over with both hands in a snapping motion using all of your fingertips and thumbs. If your hands warm up, dunk them in ice water again. Snap until your pieces of butter are about pea-size, and butter is equally covered in flour. Be careful not to overdo it. It's better to have some larger pieces than overworked butter.

LAMINATED BISCUITS HOW-TO

2 Pat dough out with your fingertips instead of using a rolling pin. Biscuit dough is already stiff, and using a rolling pin will toughen it even more. Rolling also makes your biscuits flatter.

3 When cutting biscuits, push the cutter into the dough using a straight up-and-down motion. Twisting the cutter in the dough will cause biscuits to come out lopsided.

4 Use a pastry brush to lightly paint the top of each unbaked biscuit with several swipes of melted butter.

ANGEL BISCUITS

Angel biscuits are made with a combination of yeast and chemical leavening, which makes them basically foolproof. These biscuits are tall, buttery, and dangerously light.

Makes 15 to 20

2	tablespoons (24 grams) granulated sugar
1½	tablespoons (22.5 grams) warm water (105°F/41°C to 110°F/43°C)
1	teaspoon (3 grams) active dry yeast
2¾	cups (344 grams) all-purpose flour
2	teaspoons (6 grams) kosher salt
½	teaspoon (2.5 grams) baking soda
½	teaspoon (2.5 grams) baking powder
¼	cup (57 grams) all-vegetable shortening, cubed
¼	cup (57 grams) cold unsalted butter, cubed
1	cup (240 grams) whole buttermilk
2	tablespoons (28 grams) unsalted butter, melted

1. Line a baking sheet with parchment paper.

2. In a small bowl, stir together sugar, 1½ tablespoons (22.5 grams) warm water, and yeast. Let stand until mixture is foamy, about 5 minutes.

3. In a medium bowl, whisk together flour, salt, baking soda, and baking powder. Using your fingers, cut in shortening and cold butter until mixture is crumbly. Add yeast mixture and buttermilk, stirring just until dry ingredients are moistened.

4. Turn out dough onto a lightly floured surface. Pat dough to 1-inch thickness. Using a 2½-inch round cutter, cut dough, re-patting scraps as necessary. Place on prepared pan. Cover and let rise in a warm, draft-free place (75°F/24°C) until puffed, 30 minutes to 1 hour.

5. Preheat oven to 400°F (200°C).

6. Brush biscuits with melted butter, and bake until golden brown, 12 to 15 minutes. Let cool on pan for 5 minutes. Serve warm.

POTATO ROLLS

Everyone at the table will be reaching for one of these tender, fluffy rolls that pair well with almost any dish.

Makes 24

2   medium russet potatoes (128 grams),
    peeled and cut into 1-inch pieces
1   tablespoon (9 grams) active dry yeast
½   cup (100 grams) granulated sugar, divided
7 to 7½ cups (875 to 938 grams) all-purpose flour, divided
¼   cup (57 grams) unsalted butter, softened
2   tablespoons (18 grams) kosher salt
1   tablespoon (15 grams) fresh lemon juice
2   large eggs (100 grams)
Melted unsalted butter
Flaked sea salt

1. In a large saucepan, bring potatoes and water to cover to a boil over medium-high heat; cook until tender, 10 to 12 minutes. Drain, reserving 2 cups liquid. Press potatoes through a potato ricer, and let cool completely.

2. In the bowl of a stand mixer fitted with the paddle attachment, combine 2 cups reserved potato water (110°F/43°C), yeast, and 2 teaspoons (8 grams) sugar. Let stand until mixture is foamy, about 5 minutes. Stir in mashed potatoes, 3 cups (375 grams) flour, softened butter, kosher salt, lemon juice, eggs, and remaining sugar; beat at medium speed until smooth. Gradually add remaining 4 to 4½ cups (500 to 563 grams) flour, beating until a soft dough forms.

3. Turn out dough onto a heavily floured surface, and knead until smooth and elastic, 2 to 3 minutes, sprinkling surface with additional flour as needed. Spray a large bowl with cooking spray. Place dough in bowl, turning to grease top. Cover and let rise in a warm, draft-free place (75°F/24°C), until doubled in size, about 2 hours.

4. Line a baking sheet with parchment paper, and spray with cooking spray.

5. Divide dough into 24 equal pieces. Roll each piece into a ball. Place on prepared pan. Cover and let stand in a warm, draft-free place (75°F/24°C) until puffed, about 45 minutes.

6. Preheat oven to 350°F (180°C).

7. Bake until golden brown, 25 to 30 minutes. Brush with melted butter, and sprinkle with flaked salt.

BREAD ROLLS

For the perfect appetizer, stuff these simple rolls with sliced ham and turkey, and serve with a smear of softened butter. You can also top them with an array of seeds to complement the season. Poppy seeds and sesame seeds are our favorites, but pumpkin, fennel, and cumin work just as well.

Makes 25 (2-ounce) rolls or 50 (1-ounce) rolls

2¼   cups (540 grams) warm whole milk (105°F/41°C to 110°F/43°C)
1   tablespoon (9 grams) active dry yeast
½   cup (100 grams) granulated sugar, divided
7 to 7½ cups (889 to 953 grams) bread flour, divided
¼   cup (57 grams) unsalted butter, softened
1½   tablespoons (13.5 grams) kosher salt
1   tablespoon (15 grams) fresh lemon juice
2   large eggs (100 grams)
2   large egg whites (60 grams), lightly beaten
Sesame seeds or poppy seeds
¼   cup (57 grams) unsalted butter, melted

1. In the bowl of a stand mixer fitted with the paddle attachment, combine warm milk, yeast, and 2 teaspoons (8 grams) sugar. Let stand until mixture is foamy, about 5 minutes. Stir in 3 cups (381 grams) flour, softened butter, salt, lemon juice, eggs, and remaining sugar; beat at medium speed until smooth. Gradually add remaining 4 to 4½ cups (508 to 572 grams) flour, beating until a soft dough forms.

2. Turn out dough onto a heavily floured surface, and knead until smooth and elastic, 4 to 6 minutes, sprinkling surface with additional flour as needed. Spray a large bowl with cooking spray. Place dough in bowl, turning to grease top. Cover and let rise in a warm, draft-free place (75°F/24°C) until doubled in size, 1 to 1½ hours.

3. Line a baking sheet with parchment paper, and spray with cooking spray.

4. Using a 2-ounce ice cream scoop (for 25 rolls) or a 1-ounce ice cream scoop (for 50 rolls), scoop dough, and roll into balls. Place on prepared pan so rolls are barely touching. Brush top of rolls with egg whites, and sprinkle with desired seeds. Cover and let stand in a warm, draft-free place (75°F/24°C) until puffed, about 45 minutes.

5. Preheat oven to 375°F (190°C).

6. Bake until golden brown, 20 to 25 minutes. Lightly brush with melted butter.

SOUR CREAM ROLLS

The Parmesan cheese and garlic baked into these rolls add a wonderful savory note and a flavor reminiscent of garlic bread.

Makes 24

½   cup (120 grams) warm water (105°F/41°C to 110°F/43°C)
2   tablespoons (18 grams) active dry yeast
1   cup (240 grams) sour cream
½   cup (113 grams) unsalted butter, softened
½   cup (100 grams) granulated sugar
1   tablespoon (9 grams) kosher salt
2   large eggs (100 grams), lightly beaten
5½   cups (688 grams) all-purpose flour
1¾   cups (175 grams) grated Parmesan cheese, divided
2   cloves garlic (10 grams), minced
2   tablespoons (4 grams) minced fresh thyme
⅓   cup (76 grams) unsalted butter, melted
Garnish: fresh thyme leaves

1. In the bowl of a stand mixer fitted with the paddle attachment, combine ½ cup (120 grams) warm water and yeast. Let stand until mixture is foamy, about 10 minutes.
2. In a medium saucepan, heat sour cream, softened butter, sugar, and salt over medium-low heat, stirring constantly, until butter is melted, 3 to 4 minutes. Let cool to 110°F (43°C), about 10 minutes. Whisk in eggs. With mixer on medium speed, add sour cream mixture to yeast mixture, beating until combined. Add flour, 1½ cups (150 grams) cheese, garlic, and thyme, and beat until well combined.
3. Spray a large bowl with cooking spray. Place dough in bowl, turning to grease top. Cover and let rise in a warm, draft-free place (75°F/24°C) until doubled in size, 1 to 1½ hours.

4. Spray 2 (12-cup) muffin pans with cooking spray.
5. Divide dough into 24 equal portions. Working with 1 portion at a time (keep remaining dough covered to keep from drying out), divide each portion into 3 pieces; roll each piece into a ball. Place 3 dough balls in each prepared muffin cup. Cover and let rise in a warm, draft-free place (75°F/24°C) until doubled in size, about 30 minutes.
6. Preheat oven to 350°F (180°C).
7. Bake until golden brown, 15 to 18 minutes. Brush with melted butter, and sprinkle with remaining ¼ cup (25 grams) cheese. Garnish with thyme, if desired.

HAWAIIAN BUNS

Pineapple juice gives these rolls a light, tangy sweetness that will have you saying "aloha" to this recipe time and time again.

Makes 15

4¼ cups (531 grams) all-purpose flour, divided
2 tablespoons (30 grams) warm water (105°F/41°C to 110°F/43°C)
1 tablespoon (9 grams) active dry yeast
¾ cup (180 grams) pineapple juice, canned*
⅓ cup (73 grams) firmly packed light brown sugar
¼ cup (57 grams) unsalted butter, softened
2 large eggs (100 grams)
1 large egg yolk (19 grams)
1 teaspoon (4 grams) vanilla extract
2 teaspoons (6 grams) kosher salt
Melted unsalted butter

1. In the bowl of a stand mixer fitted with the whisk attachment, combine ¼ cup (31 grams) flour, 2 tablespoons (30 grams) warm water, and yeast. Let stand until mixture is foamy, about 15 minutes. With mixer on medium speed, add pineapple juice, brown sugar, softened butter, eggs, egg yolk, and vanilla, beating until well combined.
2. In a large bowl, combine salt and remaining 4 cups (500 grams) flour. Gradually add flour mixture to pineapple mixture, beating until dough is smooth but sticky. Switch to the dough hook attachment; beat at low speed for 5 minutes. Spray a large bowl with cooking spray. Place dough in bowl, turning to grease top. Cover and let rise in a warm, draft-free place (75°F/24°C) until doubled in size, about 2 hours.

3. Line a 13x9-inch rimmed baking pan with parchment paper, and spray with cooking spray.
4. Gently punch dough down, and divide into 15 equal portions. Roll into balls. Place on prepared pan. Cover and let stand in a warm, draft-free place (75°F/24°C) until puffed, about 1 hour.
5. Preheat oven to 350°F (180°C).
6. Bake until golden brown, 20 to 25 minutes. Brush with melted butter.

*If using fresh pineapple juice, heat the juice to 200°F (93°C). Then cool to lukewarm.

PRO TIP
This dough is spongy and should not be overworked when rolling into balls. If overworked, the dough won't rise well.

PARKER HOUSE POCKET ROLLS

This is the the only dinner roll recipe you'll ever need. The Parker House Pocket Rolls use rounds of dough folded over into tidy pockets to create half-circle bites of buttery perfection.

Makes about 50 pocket rolls

Parker House Roll Dough (recipe follows)
¼ cup (57 grams) unsalted butter, melted
8 tablespoons plus 1 teaspoon (117 grams) unsalted butter, softened and cut into 50 cubes
Maldon or sea salt

1. On a lightly floured surface, turn out Parker House Roll Dough. Divide dough in half, and gently shape each half into a ball. Cover and let rest for 10 minutes.
2. Preheat oven to 375°F (190°C). Line a baking sheet with parchment paper.
3. Roll one half of dough into a 14x12-inch rectangle, about ¼ inch thick. Using a 2½-inch round cutter, cut dough, rerolling scraps as necessary. Repeat with remaining dough. Brush each circle with melted butter, and place one cube of softened butter on bottom half of each one. Fold circles over, and press to seal. Place pockets, overlapping, on prepared pan. Cover and let rise in a warm, draft-free place (75°F/24°C) until puffed, about 30 minutes.
4. Brush rolls with melted butter, and bake until golden brown, 20 to 25 minutes. Brush with melted butter again, and sprinkle with salt.

Parker House Roll Dough
Makes about 50 pocket rolls

1½ cups (360 grams) warm whole milk (105°F/41°C to 110°F/43°C), divided
¼ cup (50 grams) granulated sugar
2 teaspoons (6 grams) active dry yeast
4½ to 5 cups (563 to 625 grams) all-purpose flour, divided
6 tablespoons (84 grams) unsalted butter, melted
2 large eggs (100 grams)
2 teaspoons (6 grams) kosher salt

1. In a small bowl, whisk together ½ cup (120 grams) warm milk, sugar, and yeast. Let stand until mixture is foamy, about 10 minutes. Stir ½ cup (63 grams) flour into yeast mixture.

2. In the bowl of a stand mixer fitted with the dough hook attachment, beat melted butter, eggs, and remaining 1 cup (240 grams) warm milk at low speed until combined. Add yeast mixture, beating to combine. Add 1 cup (125 grams) flour and salt; beat to combine. Gradually add remaining flour, 1 cup (125 grams) at a time, beating until dough comes together and begins to pull away from sides of bowl, 2 to 3 minutes. (Dough will be sticky but not unmanageable. If dough is too sticky, add more flour, ¼ cup [31 grams] at a time, until it comes together.)
3. Spray a large bowl with cooking spray. Place dough in bowl, turning to grease top. Cover and let rise in a warm, draft-free place (75°F/24°C) until doubled in size, 2 to 2½ hours.

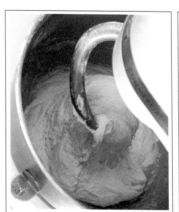

PRO TIP
Stop working the dough as soon as it comes together in your mixer. This particular dough gets handled quite a bit throughout the shaping process, so you don't want to overwork it in the initial mixing steps.

PRO TIP
Butter is the key to success with Parker House rolls—you add more at nearly every step of the process. Be sure to use unsalted butter so you have control over exactly how much salt ends up in the recipe.

DILL AND GRUYÈRE PARKER HOUSE ROUND ROLLS

The Parker House roll is the most versatile for dressing up with different flavors. Dill and Gruyère make a perfect pair in this buttery bread.

Makes about 25 round rolls

Dill and Gruyère Parker House Roll Dough (recipe follows)
¼   cup plus ½ teaspoon (59.5 grams) unsalted butter, softened and cut into 25 cubes
¼   cup (57 grams) unsalted butter, melted
Maldon or sea salt

1. On a lightly floured surface, turn out Dill and Gruyère Parker House Roll Dough. Divide dough in half, and gently shape each half into a ball. Cover and let rest for 10 minutes.
2. Line a baking sheet with parchment paper.
3. Divide dough into 25 pieces (about 1.6 ounces each). Press one cube of softened butter into center of each piece of dough, and roll into balls. Place rolls on prepared pan, leaving no space between. Cover and let rise in a warm, draft-free place (75°F/24°C) until puffed, about 30 minutes.
4. Preheat oven to 375°F (190°C).
5. Brush rolls with melted butter, and bake until golden brown, 25 to 30 minutes. Brush with melted butter again, and sprinkle with salt.

Dɪʟʟ ᴀɴᴅ Gʀᴜʏèʀᴇ Pᴀʀᴋᴇʀ Hᴏᴜsᴇ Rᴏʟʟ Dᴏᴜɢʜ

Makes about 25 round rolls

1½   cups (360 grams) warm whole milk (105°F/41°C to 110°F/43°C), divided
¼   cup (50 grams) granulated sugar
2   teaspoons (6 grams) active dry yeast
4½ to 5 cups (563 to 625 grams) all-purpose flour, divided
6   tablespoons (84 grams) unsalted butter, melted
2   large eggs (100 grams)
6   ounces (175 grams) Gruyère cheese, finely grated
½   cup (16 grams) chopped fresh dill
2   teaspoons (6 grams) kosher salt

1. In a small bowl, whisk together ½ cup (120 grams) warm milk, sugar, and yeast. Let stand until mixture is foamy, about 10 minutes. Stir ½ cup (63 grams) flour into yeast mixture.
2. In the bowl of a stand mixer fitted with the dough hook attachment, beat melted butter, eggs, and remaining 1 cup (240 grams) warm milk at low speed until combined. Add yeast mixture, beating to combine. Add 1 cup (125 grams) flour, Gruyère, dill, and salt; beat to combine. Gradually add remaining flour, 1 cup (125 grams) at a time, beating until dough comes together and begins to pull away from sides of bowl, 2 to 3 minutes. (Dough will be sticky but not unmanageable. If dough is too sticky, add more flour, ¼ cup [31 grams] at a time, until it comes together.)
3. Spray a large bowl with cooking spray. Place dough in bowl, turning to grease top. Cover and let rise in a warm, draft-free place (75°F/24°C) until doubled in size, 2 to 2½ hours.

RYE SANDWICH BREAD

We love this loaf because of its unbeatable texture, deep rye flavor, and versatility. It can be baked in a standard loaf pan, a Pullman pan, or hand-shaped into a rustic boule. This kind of versatility makes a perfect starter loaf for the timid baker!

Makes 1 (9x5-inch) loaf

2¼	cups (281 grams) all-purpose flour
1	cup (102 grams) light rye flour
1	cup (240 grams) warm whole milk (85°F/29°C)
¼	cup (85 grams) unsulphered molasses
2	tablespoons (28 grams) unsalted butter, softened
1	tablespoon (9 grams) caraway seeds
2	teaspoons (6 grams) kosher salt
2	teaspoons (6 grams) active dry yeast
1	large egg (50 grams)
1	tablespoon (15 grams) water

1. In the bowl of a stand mixer fitted with the dough hook attachment, combine flours, warm milk, molasses, butter, caraway seeds, salt, and yeast until moistened. Let stand for 20 minutes.

2. Knead for 8 minutes in mixer, or 12 minutes by hand. Spray a large bowl with cooking spray. Place dough in bowl, turning to grease top. Cover and let rise in a warm, draft-free place (75°F/24°C) until doubled in size, 1 to 2 hours.

3. Turn out dough onto a lightly floured surface, and punch down dough. Pull four corners of dough into center, and gently roll with palms to form a loaf.

4. Spray a 9x5-inch loaf pan or Pullman pan with cooking spray. Place loaf in prepared pan. Cover and let rise in a warm, draft-free place (75°F/24°C) until doubled in size, 1 to 1½ hours.

5. Preheat oven to 375°F (190°C).

6. In a small bowl, whisk together egg and 1 tablespoon (15 grams) water. Brush egg wash onto loaf, and sprinkle with additional caraway seeds, if desired. Using a sharp knife or lame, make 4 large slashes across top of loaf.

7. Bake until golden brown and an instant-read thermometer inserted in center registers 190°F (88°C), 35 to 40 minutes. Let cool in pan for 20 minutes. Remove from pan, and let cool completely on a wire rack.

PRO TIP
Don't put the lid on a Pullman loaf pan until it has finished its final rise, especially if you are new to baking with them. You may want to check on the bread while it's rising, and removing the lid will wreak havoc with the loaf. Once the dough has risen to within ½ inch of the rim of the pan, slide the lid on and bake it.

PRO TIP
With the addition of molasses, the dough for our Rye Sandwich Bread may be somewhat sticky, but resist the urge to knead in more flour as you would with wheat bread. For a tender loaf with a fine crumb, embrace the stickiness.

MARBLED RYE BREAD

Simpler than it looks, this marbled loaf is as delicious as it is beautiful. A tight, tender crumb makes it the perfect sandwich loaf. You really can't go wrong, though, simply toasting a slice, smearing it with butter, and letting its delicate rye flavor shine through.

Makes 1 (9x5-inch) loaf

4	cups (500 grams) all-purpose flour, divided
1½	cups (154 grams) rye flour, divided
6	tablespoons (84 grams) unsalted butter, softened and divided
1	tablespoon (21 grams) honey
1	tablespoon (9 grams) kosher salt, divided
2	teaspoons (6 grams) active dry yeast, divided
2	cups (480 grams) plus 1 tablespoon (15 grams) room temperature water, divided
3	tablespoons (15 grams) unsweetened cocoa powder
1	tablespoon (21 grams) unsulphered molasses
1	large egg (50 grams)
1	tablespoon (9 grams) caraway seeds
1	teaspoon (3 grams) flax seeds

1. In the bowl of a stand mixer fitted with the dough hook attachment, combine 2 cups (250 grams) all-purpose flour, ¾ cup (77 grams) rye flour, 3 tablespoons (42 grams) butter, honey, ½ tablespoon (4.5 grams) salt, and 1 teaspoon (3 grams) yeast. With mixer on medium speed, gradually add 1 cup (240 grams) water, beating until a soft dough forms. Turn out dough onto a lightly floured surface, and knead until smooth and elastic, about 10 minutes.

2. In the bowl of a stand mixer fitted with the dough hook attachment, combine cocoa, molasses, remaining 2 cups (250 grams) all-purpose flour, remaining ¾ cup (77 grams) rye flour, remaining 3 tablespoons (42 grams) butter, remaining ½ tablespoon (4.5 grams) salt, and remaining 1 teaspoon (3 grams) yeast. With mixer on medium speed, gradually add 1 cup (240 grams) water, beating until a soft dough forms. Turn out dough onto a lightly floured surface, and knead until smooth and elastic, about 10 minutes.

3. Shape each mass of dough into a ball. Spray 2 large bowls with cooking spray. Place dough in bowls, turning to grease tops. Cover and let rise in a warm, draft-free place (75°F/24°C) until doubled in size, about 1 hour.

4. Turn out dough onto a lightly floured surface, and punch dough down. Divide each ball in half. Roll each dough quarter into a 9x6-inch rectangle. Layer rectangles on top of one another, alternating light and dark. Starting at one long side, roll dough into a log.

5. Spray a 9x5-inch loaf pan with cooking spray. Place loaf, seam side down, in prepared pan. Cover and let rise in a warm, draft-free place (75°F/24°C) until doubled in size, about 1 hour.

6. Preheat oven to 375°F (190°C).

7. In a small bowl, whisk together egg and remaining 1 tablespoon (15 grams) water. Brush egg wash onto loaf. Using a sharp knife or lame, make 4 deep slashes across top of loaf. Sprinkle with caraway seeds and flax seeds.

8. Bake until golden brown and an instant-read thermometer inserted in center registers 190°F (88°C), 35 to 40 minutes. Let cool in pan for 20 minutes. Remove from pan, and let cool completely on a wire rack.

PRO TIP
To assemble our Marbled Rye Bread loaf, divide dough into quarters—two light and two dark. (We recommend weighing the dough quarters for accuracy.) Then roll out each quarter into a 9x6-inch rectangle. Stack them, alternating light and dark layers, and roll up like a jelly roll.

ROSEMARY-CHEESE DUTCH OVEN BREAD

This cheesy, herbaceous take on Dutch oven bread will be a new favorite at the dinner table.

Makes 1 (2-pound) loaf

4½   cups (563 grams) all-purpose flour
1   tablespoon (9 grams) kosher salt
½   teaspoon (1.5 grams) active dry yeast
1¼   cups (125 grams) grated Gruyère cheese, divided
1   tablespoon (2 grams) chopped fresh rosemary
1   teaspoon (2 grams) ground black pepper
2¼   cups (540 grams) warm water (105°F/41°C to 110°F/43°C)
⅓   cup (50 grams) plain yellow cornmeal

1. In a large bowl, stir together flour, salt, and yeast. Add 1 cup (100 grams) Gruyère, rosemary, and pepper, stirring until combined. Add 2¼ cups (540 grams) warm water, stirring by hand until a sticky dough forms. Cover and let rise in a warm, draft-free place (75°F/24°C) overnight or up to 24 hours.
2. On a lightly floured surface, pat dough into a circle. (This is a wet dough.) Fold four edges in toward center; turn dough smooth side up. Sprinkle with flour. Cover and let rise in a warm, draft-free place (75°F/24°C) for 2 hours.
3. Place a 4- to 6-quart cast-iron Dutch oven in cold oven. Preheat oven to 500°F (260°C).
4. Sprinkle top of dough generously with cornmeal. Using a large spatula, turn dough over; sprinkle with remaining cornmeal. Place dough in preheated Dutch oven. (Use a wooden spoon to gently push dough into bottom of pan, if necessary.)
5. Cover and bake for 30 minutes. Remove from oven, and sprinkle with remaining ¼ cup (25 grams) Gruyère. Bake, uncovered, 15 to 20 minutes more. Let cool completely on a wire rack.

MULTIGRAIN-TOPPED DUTCH OVEN BREAD

The charm of this boule is its toothsome and nutty topping. Oats, seeds, minced onion, and wheat bran pump up the crunch and the wholesome flavor.

Makes 1 (2-pound) loaf

4½ cups (563 grams) all-purpose flour
1   tablespoon (9 grams) kosher salt
½   teaspoon (1.5 grams) active dry yeast
2¼ cups (540 grams) warm water (105°F/41°C to 110°F/43°C)
3   tablespoons (27 grams) raw sunflower seeds
1   tablespoon (5 grams) old-fashioned oats
1   tablespoon (6 grams) dried minced onion
1   tablespoon (4 grams) wheat bran
2   teaspoons (6 grams) coarse sea salt
1   teaspoon (3 grams) poppy seeds
1   teaspoon (3 grams) sesame seeds
1   teaspoon (3 grams) flax seeds

1. In a large bowl, stir together flour, kosher salt, and yeast. Add 2¼ cups (540 grams) warm water, and stir by hand until a sticky dough forms. Cover and let rise in a warm, draft-free place (75°F/24°C) overnight or up to 24 hours.
2. On a lightly floured surface, pat dough into a circle. (This is a wet dough.) Fold four edges in toward center; turn dough smooth side up. Sprinkle with flour. Cover and let rise in a warm, draft-free place (75°F/24°C) for 2 hours.
3. Place a 4- to 6-quart cast-iron Dutch oven in cold oven. Preheat oven to 500°F (260°C).
4. In a small bowl, stir together sunflower seeds, oats, onion, wheat bran, sea salt, poppy seeds, sesame seeds, and flax seeds. Sprinkle top of dough generously with mixture. Place dough in preheated Dutch oven. (Use a wooden spoon to gently push dough into bottom of pan, if necessary.)
5. Cover and bake for 30 minutes. Uncover and bake 15 to 20 minutes more. Let cool completely on a wire rack.

CRANBERRY-PECAN DUTCH OVEN BREAD

A staple of the autumn bread basket, this cranberry- and pecan-studded loaf is a hearty treat to enjoy on cool fall nights.

Makes 1 (2-pound) loaf

3   cups (375 grams) all-purpose flour
1½   cups (195 grams) whole wheat flour
1   tablespoon (9 grams) kosher salt
½   teaspoon (1.5 grams) active dry yeast
1   cup (128 grams) dried cranberries
1   cup (113 grams) chopped pecans
1½   teaspoons (3 grams) ground cinnamon
2¼   cups (540 grams) warm water (105°F/41°C to 110°F/43°C)
⅓   cup (50 grams) plain yellow cornmeal

1. In a large bowl, stir together flours, salt, and yeast. Add cranberries, pecans, and cinnamon, stirring until combined. Add 2¼ cups (540 grams) warm water, and stir by hand until a sticky dough forms. Cover and let rise in a warm, draft-free place (75°F/24°C) overnight or up to 24 hours.
2. On a lightly floured surface, pat dough into a circle. (This is a wet dough.) Fold four edges in toward center; turn dough smooth side up. Sprinkle with flour. Cover and let rise in a warm, draft-free place (75°F/24°C) for 2 hours.
3. Place a 4- to 6-quart cast-iron Dutch oven in cold oven. Preheat oven to 500°F (260°C).
4. Sprinkle top of dough generously with cornmeal. Using a large spatula, turn dough over; sprinkle with remaining cornmeal. Place dough in preheated Dutch oven. (Use a wooden spoon to gently push dough into bottom of pan, if necessary.)
5. Cover and bake for 30 minutes. Uncover and bake 15 to 20 minutes more. Let cool completely on a wire rack.

DUTCH OVEN BREAD BAKING TIPS

BAKING TIPS

It doesn't matter if you use an enamel-coated cast-iron Dutch oven or a traditional black cast-iron Dutch oven. As long as you have a lid to cover it, the bread comes out perfectly every time. We found that using a 4- to 6-quart Dutch oven yields the perfectly round shape.

Fight the urge to grease your Dutch oven. Because of the high temperature, the fat will burn off almost immediately, giving your bread a charred taste.

Splurge for high-quality ingredients—especially flour. The better the flour, the tastier your bread will be.

Make these recipes your own! You can easily substitute different cheeses, herbs, dried fruits, and nuts to create your own signature loaves.

MINI BRIOCHE À TÊTE

These are perfect for breakfast. We like to pluck the têtes off and spoon scoops of frozen granita, seasonal jam, or hazelnut spread, such as Nutella, in the remaining brioche.

Makes 12

Basic Brioche Dough (recipe follows)
1   large egg (50 grams), lightly beaten

1. Butter and flour 12 (3-inch) brioche à tête molds. Line a baking sheet with parchment paper.
2. Divide Basic Brioche Dough into 12 (60-gram) balls and 12 (20-gram) balls. Place large balls in prepared molds and small balls on prepared pan. Cover and let rise in a warm, draft-free place (75°F/24°C) until dough is puffed, 30 to 40 minutes.
3. Preheat oven to 400°F (200°C).
4. Using your thumbs, make a deep indentation in center of each large ball. Place smaller balls into wells, and brush with egg wash.
5. Bake for 10 minutes. Reduce oven temperature to 350°F (180°C), and bake until golden brown and an instant-read thermometer inserted in center registers 190°F (88°C), about 12 minutes more.

BASIC BRIOCHE DOUGH
Makes 12 brioche à tête

⅓   cup (80 grams) warm whole milk (80°F/27°C to 100°F/38°C)
3   tablespoons (36 grams) granulated sugar
1   tablespoon (9 grams) active dry yeast
3¼   cups (406 grams) all-purpose flour, divided
5   large eggs (250 grams), room temperature
1   teaspoon (3 grams) kosher salt
1   cup (227 grams) unsalted butter, softened

1. In the bowl of a stand mixer fitted with the paddle attachment, combine warm milk, sugar, and yeast. Let stand until mixture is foamy, about 10 minutes.
2. Add 1½ cups (188 grams) flour and eggs, and beat at medium-low speed until smooth, 2 to 3 minutes. Cover and let stand for 30 to 45 minutes.

3. Switch to the dough hook attachment. Add salt and remaining 1¾ cups (218 grams) flour, and beat at medium speed until a smooth and elastic dough forms and pulls away from sides of bowl, 8 to 10 minutes.
4. With mixer on medium speed, add butter, 1 tablespoon (14 grams) at a time, letting each piece incorporate before adding the next. Spray a large bowl with cooking spray. Place dough in bowl, turning to grease top. Cover and let rise in a warm, draft-free place (75°F/24°C) until doubled in size, 1½ to 2½ hours.
5. On a lightly floured surface, turn out dough, and fold a few times to knock out a bit of air. Return dough to greased bowl; cover and refrigerate for at least 8 hours or overnight.

PRO TIP
When making brioche, the quality of the butter matters. This is the time to splurge on a good, high-fat butter, such as Kerrygold.

PRO TIP
To make a **Sugar-Dusted Brioche au Sucre**, divide Basic Brioche Dough into 12 (80-gram) portions, shape them into balls, brush with egg wash, and sprinkle with pearl sugar. Bake as directed in step 5 of Mini Brioche à Tête recipe.

BRIOCHE AU CHOCOLAT LOAF

Adding dark chocolate to basic brioche gives it a rich, satisfying twist that feels just as at home on the breakfast table as the dessert plate.

Makes 1 (9x5-inch) loaf

Basic Brioche Dough (recipe follows)
¾ cup (128 grams) chopped 64% cacao dark chocolate
1 large egg (50 grams), lightly beaten

1. Butter and flour a 9x5-inch loaf pan.
2. On a lightly floured surface, turn out Basic Brioche Dough. Punch down dough, and sprinkle chocolate onto dough. Knead chocolate into dough briefly, just until chocolate is incorporated. Shape dough into a loaf. Place dough, seam side down, in prepared pan. Cover and let rise in a warm, draft-free place (75°F/24°C) until dough is puffed, 30 to 40 minutes.
3. Preheat oven to 400°F (200°C).
4. Brush top of loaf with egg wash, and bake for 15 minutes. Reduce oven temperature to 350°F (180°C), and bake until golden brown and an instant-read thermometer inserted in center registers 190°F (88°C), 35 to 40 minutes more.

BASIC BRIOCHE DOUGH

Makes 1 (9x5-inch) loaf

⅓ cup (80 grams) warm whole milk (80°F/27°C to 100°F/38°C)
¼ cup (50 grams) granulated sugar
1 tablespoon (9 grams) active dry yeast
3¼ cups (406 grams) all-purpose flour, divided
5 large eggs (250 grams), room temperature
1 teaspoon (3 grams) kosher salt
1 cup (227 grams) unsalted butter, softened

1. In the bowl of a stand mixer fitted with the paddle attachment, combine warm milk, sugar, and yeast. Let stand until mixture is foamy, about 10 minutes.
2. With mixer on medium-low speed, add 1½ cups (188 grams) flour and eggs, beating until smooth, 2 to 3 minutes. Cover and let stand for 30 to 45 minutes.

3. Switch to the dough hook attachment. Add salt and remaining 1¾ cups (218 grams) flour, and beat at medium speed until a smooth and elastic dough forms and pulls away from sides of bowl, 8 to 10 minutes.
4. With mixer on medium speed, add butter, 1 tablespoon (14 grams) at a time, letting each piece incorporate before adding the next. Spray a large bowl with cooking spray. Place dough in bowl, turning to grease top. Cover and let rise in a warm, draft-free place (75°F/24°C) until doubled in size, 1½ to 2½ hours.
5. On a lightly floured surface, turn out dough, and fold a few times to knock out a bit of air. Return dough to greased bowl; cover and refrigerate for at least 8 hours or overnight.

PRO TIP
Mixing really matters. Proper mixing is what gives brioche its soft, feathery finish. Be sure to let every pat of butter fully incorporate before adding more (step 4 in Basic Brioche Dough). Don't rush it.

CHEESE AND ROSEMARY BRIOCHE

We love this recipe for sandwich bread or an afternoon snack. Though the recipe calls for a double-cream cheese, we especially love this with the ultra-rich and creamy Saint André triple-cream cow's milk cheese.

Makes 2 (9x5-inch) loaves

Basic Brioche Dough (recipe follows)
10.5   ounces (315 grams) double-cream cheese, cubed
2   tablespoons (4 grams) chopped fresh rosemary
1   large egg (50 grams)
1   tablespoon (15 grams) water

1. Make Basic Brioche Dough as directed through step 4. Place dough on a lightly floured surface, and fold in cheese and rosemary. Continue following Basic Brioche Dough recipe as directed.
2. Butter and flour 2 (9x5-inch) loaf pans.
3. Divide dough into 6 equal pieces. On a lightly floured surface, roll each piece into a 12-inch-long rope. Braid 3 pieces of dough very tightly. Place in 1 prepared pan, folding ends of braid under to fit in pan. Repeat procedure with remaining 3 pieces of dough and second prepared pan. Cover and let rise in a warm, draft-free place (75°F/24°C) until doubled in size, 1 to 1½ hours.
4. Preheat oven to 350°F (180°C).
5. In a small bowl, whisk together egg and 1 tablespoon (15 grams) water. Brush top of loaves with egg wash.
6. Bake for 30 minutes. Cover with foil, and bake until an instant-read thermometer inserted in center registers 190°F (88°C), 15 to 20 minutes more. Serve warm.

BASIC BRIOCHE DOUGH
Makes 2 (9x5-inch) loaves

⅓   cup (80 grams) warm whole milk (80°F/27°C to 100°F/38°C)
3   tablespoons (36 grams) granulated sugar
1   tablespoon (9 grams) active dry yeast
3¼   cups (406 grams) all-purpose flour, divided
5   large eggs (250 grams), room temperature
1   teaspoon (3 grams) kosher salt
1   cup (227 grams) unsalted butter, softened

1. In the bowl of a stand mixer fitted with the paddle attachment, combine warm milk, sugar, and yeast. Let stand until mixture is foamy, about 10 minutes.
2. Add 1½ cups (188 grams) flour and eggs, and beat at medium-low speed until smooth, 2 to 3 minutes. Cover and let stand for 30 to 45 minutes.
3. Switch to the dough hook attachment. Add salt and remaining 1¾ cups (218 grams) flour, and beat at medium speed until a smooth and elastic dough forms and pulls away from sides of bowl, 8 to 10 minutes.
4. With mixer on medium speed, add butter, 1 tablespoon (14 grams) at a time, letting each piece incorporate before adding the next. Spray a large bowl with cooking spray. Place dough in bowl, turning to grease top. Cover and let rise in a warm, draft-free place (75°F/24°C) until doubled in size, 1½ to 2½ hours.
5. On a lightly floured surface, turn out dough, and fold a few times to knock out a bit of air. Return dough to greased bowl; cover and refrigerate for at least 8 hours or overnight.

Photo by Stephen DeVries

SWEET POTATO BRIOCHE WITH ORANGE-PECAN STREUSEL

This brioche will knock your socks off. Incorporating streusel into the body of this lightly sweetened loaf infuses the bread with a subtle orange essence. It is absolutely worth the effort.

Makes 2 (9x5-inch) loaves

1	large or 2 small sweet potatoes (493 grams)
½	cup (120 grams) warm water (105°F/41°C to 110°F/43°C)
½	cup (100 grams) plus ⅓ cup (67 grams) granulated sugar, divided
3	tablespoons (27 grams) active dry yeast
7½	cups (938 grams) all-purpose flour, divided
5	large eggs (250 grams), divided
4	teaspoons (12 grams) kosher salt, divided
1	cup (227 grams) unsalted butter, softened
1	cup (113 grams) finely chopped pecans
⅓	cup (73 grams) firmly packed light brown sugar
2	tablespoons (6 grams) orange zest
½	cup (113 grams) unsalted butter, melted

1. Preheat oven to 400°F (200°C). Line a baking sheet with foil.
2. Scrub sweet potatoes, pat dry, and pierce several times with a fork. Bake until tender, about 1 hour. Let cool for 10 minutes. Peel sweet potatoes, and mash pulp with a fork. Set aside.
3. In the bowl of a stand mixer fitted with the paddle attachment, combine ½ cup (120 grams) warm water, ¼ cup (50 grams) granulated sugar, and yeast. Let stand until mixture is foamy, about 10 minutes.
4. Add 1⅓ cups (167 grams) flour and 1 egg (50 grams), and beat at low speed until smooth, 2 to 3 minutes. Cover and let rise until doubled in size, 30 to 45 minutes.

5. Add sweet potato purée, 4½ cups (563 grams) flour, ¼ cup (50 grams) granulated sugar, 3 eggs (150 grams), and 3 teaspoons (9 grams) salt; beat at low speed until combined, stopping to scrape sides of bowl. Increase mixer speed to medium, and beat until dough is smooth and elastic, 2 to 3 minutes.
6. With mixer on medium speed, add softened butter, 1 tablespoon (14 grams) at a time, letting each piece incorporate before adding the next. Spray a large bowl with cooking spray. Place dough in bowl, turning to grease top. Cover and let rise in a warm, draft-free place (75°F/24°C) until doubled in size, about 2 hours.
7. In a medium bowl, whisk together pecans, brown sugar, zest, remaining 1⅔ cups (208 grams) flour, remaining ⅓ cup (67 grams) granulated sugar, and remaining 1 teaspoon (3 grams) salt. Drizzle with melted butter, and stir with a wooden spoon until combined. Crumble with your fingertips until desired consistency is reached. Set aside.
8. Preheat oven to 350°F (180°C). Spray 2 (9x5-inch) loaf pans with cooking spray, and line pans with parchment paper.
9. Turn out dough onto a lightly floured surface. Punch down dough, and divide in half. Loosely cover and let rest for 10 minutes. Roll half of dough into a 16x9-inch rectangle. Sprinkle with one-fourth of streusel. Starting with one short side, roll up dough, jelly roll style, and press seam to seal. Place dough, seam side down, in prepared pan. Repeat with remaining dough and one-fourth of streusel. Cover and let rise in a warm, draft-free place (75°F/24°C) for 30 to 45 minutes.
10. Brush top of loaves with remaining 1 egg (50 grams), and sprinkle with remaining streusel.
11. Bake until golden brown and an instant-read thermometer inserted in center registers 190°F (88°C), 45 minutes to 1 hour, loosely covering with foil halfway through baking to prevent excess browning, if necessary. Let cool in pans for 10 minutes. Remove from pans, and let cool completely on wire racks.

The name is no mistake: Starter is the beginning for all sourdough bread. Creating a workable sourdough starter can take anywhere from five to 12 days depending on a variety of factors, like the temperature and the availability of (good) bacteria in your kitchen. Take the time to get yours going and it will pay off for years to come—we know people who have been feeding the same starter for over three decades!

SOURDOUGH STARTER

[WHAT YOU NEED]

- A scale (highly recommended to measure both flour and water, but measuring cups will do in a pinch).
- A 2-quart container (glass or plastic) with a lid.
- Flour. We use unbleached all-purpose flour, but whole wheat also adds a nice depth of flavor to your final product.
- Water. We use tap water, but if your water at home is highly chlorinated, you can measure your water the night before using, and let it sit on the counter overnight to allow the chlorine to dissipate. If your water simply tastes bad, or you are worried about it affecting the quality of your breads, try filtered or bottled water.

[HOW TO MAKE IT]

DAY 1: HERE WE GO!

¾ cup plus 2 tablespoons (110 grams) all-purpose flour
½ cup (113 grams) water

In a 2-quart container, combine flour and ½ cup (113 grams) water, stirring to combine. Mixture will resemble thick batter. Loosely cover (with a towel or lid askew), and let stand at room temperature (about 75°F/24°C) for 24 hours. (Can you believe that's all it takes?)

DAY 2: FEED THE STARTER.

¾ cup plus 2 tablespoons (110 grams) all-purpose flour
½ cup (113 grams) water

Open up your starter, and check for tiny bubbles that may have begun to form around the top. Bubbling indicates that yeast has begun to grow. If you don't see any yet, don't fret. Weigh out flour and ½ cup (113 grams) water, and add to yesterday's mixture. Stir to combine. Starter will feel like thick dough. Loosely cover and let stand at room temperature (about 75°F/24°C) for another 24 hours.

DAY 3: FEED THE STARTER.

¾ cup plus 2 tablespoons (110 grams) all-purpose flour
½ cup (113 grams) water

By day 3, you should be seeing some activity, and your starter should start to smell tangy and—get this—sour. Measure the flour and ½ cup (113 grams) water, and combine them in your container. Loosely cover and let stand at room temperature (about 75°F/24°C) for another 24 hours.

DAY 4: FEED THE STARTER.

¾ cup plus 2 tablespoons (110 grams) all-purpose flour
½ cup (113 grams) water

By day 4, your starter might be producing lots of bubbles, large and small. It should smell pretty pungent (vinegary and yeasty). It should also appear a bit looser (not quite so thick and sticky). Measure your flour and ½ cup (113 grams) water, and add them to your container. Stir to combine, and loosely cover. Let stand at room temperature (about 75°F/24°C) for another 24 hours.

DAY 5: ARE WE THERE YET?

¾ cup plus 2 tablespoons (110 grams) all-purpose flour
½ cup (113 grams) water

Open up your starter. By day 5, there should be lots of bubbles and your starter should smell very strong. It should also appear looser and have bubbles running throughout. These are the signs that your starter is ripe and ready to use.

Once your starter is ripe, you no longer need to add bulk to it. From here on out, you will discard* about half, and feed it with flour and ½ cup (113 grams) water on a daily basis. At this point, we like to move our starter to a smaller, more manageable container (about 1 quart).

Remove 4 ounces (113 grams or ½ cup) of starter, and place it in your new, clean container, discarding the rest. Measure flour and ½ cup (113 grams) water, and add to starter, stirring to combine. Loosely cover and let stand at room temperature (about 75°F/24°C) for another 24 hours. After this, it's ready to use.

*Always discard your starter in the trash can. Pouring it down your sink will clog it up. Alternatively, you can give your starter to a friend, or use it to make pancakes or waffles.

[TO MAINTAIN YOUR STARTER]

Continue this process, discarding all but 4 ounces (113 grams or ½ cup) of starter and adding ¾ cup plus 2 tablespoons (110 grams) flour and ½ cup (113 grams) water once a day. Once your starter is well-established (after 2 weeks or so), you can keep it covered in the refrigerator and feed it weekly. Just don't forget to take it out and feed it once a week, or the starter will die, and you'll have to begin the process all over again.

SOURDOUGH BAGUETTE

These classic long loaves might seem intimidating, and they do take quite a bit of time (upwards of 10 hours), but they aren't technically difficult. For most of the time, the dough is left alone, letting the starter, flour, yeast, and water silently work their magic. The secret to success? Don't mess with the dough too much. Overmixing or overworking will give you a flat, dense loaf.

Makes 6 (16-inch) baguettes

5⅔ cups (709 grams) unbleached all-purpose flour
1½ cups (360 grams) warm water (105°F/41°C to 110°F/43°C)
1 cup (226 grams) Sourdough Starter (recipe on page 161)
1 tablespoon (9 grams) kosher salt
1 tablespoon (12 grams) granulated sugar
2 teaspoons (6 grams) active dry yeast
Semolina flour (for finishing)
2 cups (480 grams) ice water

STEP 1: MIX THE DOUGH
In the bowl of a stand mixer fitted with the dough hook attachment, beat flour, 1½ cups (360 grams) warm water, Sourdough Starter, salt, sugar, and yeast at medium speed until a smooth, elastic dough forms, about 5 minutes. (Humidity, elevation, and temperature all affect sourdough breads. If the dough appears too dry and crumbly, add more water, 1 tablespoon [15 grams] at a time.)

STEP 2: LET IT RISE
Spray a large bowl with cooking spray. Place dough in bowl, turning to grease top. Cover and let rise in a warm, draft-free place (75°F/24°C) until doubled in size, about 1 hour. Refrigerate covered bowl for at least 8 hours or overnight before proceeding.

STEP 3: SCALE THE DOUGH
Turn out dough onto a lightly oiled surface, and divide into 6 equal portions (230 to 250 grams each). Shape each piece into a 4-inch rectangle, tucking ends under, being careful not to overwork the dough. Place rectangles on a parchment paper-lined baking sheet sprinkled with semolina flour. Cover with oiled plastic wrap, and let gluten relax for 20 minutes.

STEP 4: SHAPE THE BAGUETTES
Press each rectangle firmly with the palm of your hand to de-gas. Fold top half of rectangle toward center; using your fingertips, form a seal along midline. Turn rectangle, and repeat with bottom half. Fold top third of dough down to center, and seal across seam with the palm of your hand. Repeat this process twice, pinching final seal with your fingertips. Beginning at center and moving outward, roll dough with both hands. Apply more pressure with outer edges of your hands to achieve a tapered look.

STEP 5: PROOF THE DOUGH
Place baguettes on parchment paper-lined baking sheets sprinkled with semolina. Cover with oiled plastic wrap, and let proof for 1 to 2 hours. (Proofing is the bread's final rise before it goes into the oven.) Preheat oven to 475°F (250°C). Position one oven rack to lowest level, and place one in center of oven. Place a large cast-iron skillet on bottom rack.

STEP 6: SCORE THE LOAVES
When the baguettes are puffed (but not doubled in size), sprinkle with semolina, and slash with a lame or razor blade.

STEP 7: BAKE THE LOAVES
Pour 2 cups (480 grams) ice water in cast-iron skillet, and place loaves immediately into hot oven. Bake for 15 minutes. Reduce oven temperature to 425°F (220°C), and bake until baguettes are deeply golden brown, about 10 minutes more. Remove from pan, and let cool completely on a wire rack.

Scaling, in baker's terms, means weighing out and dividing the dough. (See STEP 3.)

Scoring cuts slashes into the dough that allow steam to escape when baking. Scoring is the key to perfectly crusted bread, and different types of loaves (baguette, boule) require different kinds of scoring. (See STEP 6.)

SOURDOUGH CIABATTA

This rustic Italian loaf was first made in 1982—yes, that recently—by Arnaldo Cavallari, a baker from outside Venice who was troubled by the popularity of sandwiches made out of imported French baguettes. To save his own bakery, he came up with this soft, high-gluten loaf, full of holes that are perfect for nesting sandwich ingredients.

Makes 1 loaf

1½ cups (188 grams) unbleached all-purpose flour
1¼ cups (385 grams) Sourdough Starter (recipe on page 161)
¼ cup (60 grams) water
3 tablespoons (42 grams) olive oil
1 tablespoon (9 grams) kosher salt
1 tablespoon (8 grams) nonfat dry milk powder
1 teaspoon (4 grams) granulated sugar
1 teaspoon (3 grams) active dry yeast
Semolina flour (for finishing)

STEP 1: MIX THE DOUGH

In the bowl of a stand mixer fitted with the dough hook attachment, beat flour, Sourdough Starter, ¼ cup (60 grams) water, oil, salt, milk powder, sugar, and yeast at medium speed until a smooth and elastic dough forms, 6 to 9 minutes.

STEP 2: LET IT RISE

Spray a medium bowl with cooking spray. Place dough in bowl, turning to grease top. Cover and let rise in a warm, draft-free place (75°F/24°C) until doubled in size, 1½ to 2 hours.

STEP 3: SHAPE THE LOAF

Turn out dough onto a greased baking pan, and gently stretch into a log, folding ends under to create a large, wide loaf. Cover and let rest in a warm, draft-free place (75°F/24°C) for 1 hour.

STEP 4: DOCK THE DOUGH

Gently dock dough with your fingers, creating deep indentations all over top.

STEP 5: PROOF THE DOUGH

Cover and let rise for 1 hour.

STEP 6: BAKE THE LOAF

Preheat oven to 425°F (220°C). Sprinkle loaf with semolina flour, fill a spray bottle with water, and spritz top. Bake until golden brown, 18 to 20 minutes. Remove from the oven, and let cool on a wire rack before slicing.

PRO TIP
Docking a dough refers to the process of pressing firmly with your fingertips to create little indentations all over your bread. Ciabatta and focaccia both require docking.

BASIC FOCACCIA

Focaccia is one of those classic recipes you need to add to your repertoire—especially when you realize how straightforward it is and how simple it is to customize.

Makes 1 (14x12-inch) loaf

Basic Focaccia Dough (recipe follows)
Olive oil

1. Preheat oven to 400°F (200°C). Line a baking sheet with parchment paper, and spray with cooking spray.
2. Turn out Basic Focaccia Dough onto prepared pan. Using your fingertips, gently press dough into a 14x12-inch rectangle. Dimple dough with your fingertips.
3. Bake until golden brown, 18 to 20 minutes. Brush with oil.

BASIC FOCACCIA DOUGH
Makes 1 (14x12-inch) loaf

2¾ cups (349 grams) bread flour
1 cup (192 grams) semolina flour
2 cups (480 grams) warm water (105°F/41°C to 110°F/43°C)
1 tablespoon plus 1 teaspoon (12 grams) active dry yeast
1¼ teaspoons (3.75 grams) kosher salt
¼ cup (56 grams) olive oil

1. In the bowl of a stand mixer fitted with the dough hook attachment, beat flours and 2 cups (480 grams) warm water at low speed until combined, about 1 minute. Sprinkle yeast on top of dough, and let stand for 10 minutes.
2. Add salt, and beat at low speed until combined. Increase mixer speed to medium-high, and beat until smooth and elastic, 2 to 3 minutes. With mixer on low speed, add oil in a slow, steady stream, beating until combined, 1 to 2 minutes.
3. Spray a large bowl with cooking spray. Place dough in bowl, turning to grease top. Cover and let rise in a warm, draft-free place (75°F/24°C) until doubled in size, 1½ to 2 hours.

PRO TIP
To make **Rosemary Sea Salt Focaccia**, add ¼ cup (8 grams) chopped fresh rosemary with flours and water in step 1 when making Basic Focaccia Dough. Continue as directed. Follow directions for Basic Focaccia, and sprinkle with 1 tablespoon (9 grams) sea salt after brushing with olive oil.

FOCACCIA WITH ASIAGO, THYME & POTATO

Sweet caramelized onions are the secret to making this simple bread extraordinary.

Makes 1 (14x12-inch) loaf

4	cups (960 grams) cool water
1½	teaspoons (4.5 grams) kosher salt, divided
1	pound (455 grams) Yukon gold potatoes
3	tablespoons (42 grams) unsalted butter
1	yellow onion (400 grams), thinly sliced
½	teaspoon (1 gram) ground black pepper
	Basic Focaccia Dough (recipe follows)
¼	cup (25 grams) grated Asiago cheese
	Olive oil, for brushing
¼	cup (8 grams) fresh thyme leaves

1. In a medium bowl, stir together 4 cups (960 grams) cool water and 1 teaspoon (3 grams) salt.

2. Peel and thinly slice potatoes using a mandoline or a very sharp knife. Place sliced potatoes in saltwater solution, and refrigerate for at least 2 hours or overnight. Drain potatoes, and spread on paper towels to let dry for a few minutes.

3. In a medium skillet, melt butter over low heat. Add onion, pepper, and remaining ½ teaspoon (1.5 grams) salt; cook, stirring frequently, until onions are lightly caramelized, 20 to 30 minutes. Let cool.

4. Preheat oven to 400°F (200°C). Line a baking sheet with parchment paper, and spray with cooking spray.

5. Turn out Basic Focaccia Dough onto prepared pan. Using your fingertips, gently press dough into a 14x12-inch rectangle. Dimple dough with your fingertips. Sprinkle dough with caramelized onions, and shingle with potato slices. Sprinkle with cheese.

6. Bake until golden brown, 18 to 20 minutes. Brush with oil, and sprinkle with thyme.

BASIC FOCACCIA DOUGH

Makes 1 (14x12-inch) loaf

2¾	cups (349 grams) bread flour
1	cup (192 grams) semolina flour
2	cups (480 grams) warm water (105°F/41°C to 110°F/43°C)
1	tablespoon plus 1 teaspoon (12 grams) active dry yeast
1¼	teaspoons (3.75 grams) kosher salt
¼	cup (56 grams) olive oil

1. In the bowl of a stand mixer fitted with the dough hook attachment, beat flours and 2 cups (480 grams) warm water at low speed until combined, about 1 minute. Sprinkle yeast on top of dough, and let stand for 10 minutes.

2. Add salt, and beat at low speed until combined. Increase mixer speed to medium-high, and beat until smooth and elastic, 2 to 3 minutes. With mixer on low speed, add oil in a slow, steady stream, beating until combined, 1 to 2 minutes.

3. Spray a large bowl with cooking spray. Place dough in bowl, turning to grease top. Cover and let rise in a warm, draft-free place (75°F/24°C) until doubled in size, 1½ to 2 hours.

PRETZEL ROLLS

To help these rolls bake evenly, use a lame or a super sharp knife to slash an "X" into the top of each roll.

Makes 9

Pretzel Dough (recipe follows)
¼   cup (60 grams) baking soda
1   large egg (50 grams), lightly beaten
3   tablespoons (42 grams) unsalted butter, melted
Kosher salt or desired toppings (recipes follow)

1. Preheat oven to 400°F (200°C). Line 2 baking sheets with parchment paper, and spray with cooking spray.
2. Turn out Pretzel Dough, and divide into 9 equal pieces (about 4 ounces each). Roll each piece into a ball, and place on prepared pans. Cover and let rest for 5 to 10 minutes.
3. Bring a large pot of water to a boil over medium-high heat, and add baking soda. (Make sure pot is deep enough. Once you add baking soda, the water will expand an additional 2 inches.)
4. Slash top of each roll with a lame or very sharp blade. Drop each roll into boiling water-baking soda solution for 30 seconds per side. Remove from water using a large slotted spoon. Place back on prepared pans, and brush with egg wash.
5. Bake until golden brown, 15 to 20 minutes. Brush with melted butter, and sprinkle with salt or desired toppings.

PRETZEL DOUGH

Makes 9 rolls

1½   cups (360 grams) warm dark beer (120°F/49°C)
1   tablespoon (14 grams) firmly packed dark brown sugar
2   teaspoons (6 grams) active dry yeast
5 to 5½ cups (625 to 688 grams) all-purpose flour, divided
½   cup (120 grams) warm milk (105°F/41°C to 110°F/43°C)
2   tablespoons (16 grams) malt powder (can be diastatic or non-diastatic)
1   tablespoon (9 grams) kosher salt

1. In the bowl of a stand mixer fitted with the dough hook attachment, stir together warm beer, brown sugar, and yeast. Let stand until mixture is foamy, about 10 minutes.

2. Add 5 cups (625 grams) flour, warm milk, malt powder, and salt, and beat at low speed until combined. Increase mixer speed to medium-high, and beat until smooth and elastic, 5 to 6 minutes. Add remaining ½ cup (63 grams) flour, if needed. (Dough should not be sticky.)
3. Spray a large bowl with cooking spray. Place dough in bowl, turning to grease top. Cover and let rise in a warm, draft-free place (75°F/24°C) until doubled in size, about 1 hour.

TOPPINGS
These two spice blends are sure crowd-pleasers.

EVERYTHING SPICE BLEND

Makes about ½ cup

2   tablespoons (12 grams) garlic powder
2   tablespoons (12 grams) dried onion
2   tablespoons (18 grams) sesame seeds
2   tablespoons (18 grams) poppy seeds
1   tablespoon plus 1 teaspoon (12 grams) kosher salt

1. In a small bowl, combine all ingredients. Store in an airtight container until ready to use.

DUKKAH BLEND

Makes about 1 cup

½   cup (57 grams) pine nuts
¼   cup (36 grams) sesame seeds
2   tablespoons (18 grams) coriander seeds
2   tablespoons (18 grams) cumin seeds
2   teaspoons (6 grams) kosher salt
1   teaspoon (2 grams) turmeric
½   teaspoon (1 gram) ground black pepper

1. In a small saucepan, heat all ingredients over medium heat. Toast until fragrant, 5 to 6 minutes. Transfer to the work bowl of a food processor. Process until mixture is fine and crumbly, 30 seconds to 1 minute. Store in an airtight container until ready to use.

CARAMELIZED GARLIC ROOSTERKOEK

Taking inspiration from the heavy Indian influence on South African food, this bread is reminiscent of curry-dipped garlic naan. The addition of coconut water, freshly grated ginger, and curry gives this grill cake a heady taste of India.

Makes 1 (10-inch) loaf

¾ cup (180 grams) plus 2 tablespoons (30 grams) warm coconut water (105°F/41°C to 110°F/43°C), divided
1 tablespoon (6 grams) instant yeast
2 teaspoons (8 grams) granulated sugar
2½ cups (313 grams) all-purpose flour
1 tablespoon (2 grams) grated fresh ginger
2 teaspoons (6 grams) kosher salt
1½ teaspoons (3 grams) curry powder
2 tablespoons (28 grams) sunflower oil
Caramelized Garlic (recipe follows)

1. In a small bowl, combine 2 tablespoons (30 grams) warm coconut water, yeast, and sugar. Let stand until mixture is foamy, about 2 minutes.
2. In the bowl of a stand mixer fitted with the dough hook attachment, combine flour, ginger, salt, and curry powder. With mixer on medium-low speed, gradually add oil and remaining ¾ cup (180 grams) warm coconut water, beating until a shaggy dough forms, 1 to 2 minutes. Scrape sides of bowl, and add yeast mixture. Increase mixer speed to medium, and beat until dough is smooth, 4 to 5 minutes. Reduce mixer speed to medium-low. Add Caramelized Garlic, and beat until combined, about 2 minutes.
3. Turn out dough onto a lightly floured surface, and shape into a ball. (Dough may be sticky; use additional flour, if needed.) Spray a large bowl with cooking spray. Place dough in bowl, turning to grease top. Cover with plastic wrap, and let stand in a warm, draft-free place (75°F/24°C) until doubled in size, about 1 hour.
4. Preheat grill to medium-high heat (375°F/190°C).
5. Turn out dough onto a lightly floured surface, and shape into a 10-inch disk. Cover and let rest for 15 minutes.
6. Spray a braai grid or grill basket with cooking spray, and heat on grill for 5 minutes.
7. Grill disk in braai grid or grill basket, covered, until top of bread begins to puff and bottom is golden brown, 6 to 7 minutes. Turn, and grill 6 to 7 minutes more. Serve warm. Store in an airtight container for up to 4 days.

CARAMELIZED GARLIC

Makes about ¼ cup

6 cloves garlic (30 grams)
1 tablespoon (14 grams) olive oil
1 cup (240 grams) water
1 teaspoon (5 grams) balsamic vinegar
1 tablespoon (12 grams) granulated sugar

1. In a small saucepan, bring garlic and water to cover by 1 inch to a simmer over medium heat. Simmer for 3 minutes. Drain, and return cloves to pan. Increase heat to medium-high, and add oil; cook until cloves are golden, about 2 minutes. Remove from heat, and let cool for 5 minutes.
2. Slowly add 1 cup (240 grams) water and vinegar, and bring to a simmer over medium heat; simmer for 5 minutes. Add sugar, and cook, stirring constantly, until garlic is coated in a dark caramelized syrup, 3 to 5 minutes. Let cool completely. Refrigerate in an airtight container for up to 1 week.

STOLLEN

This buttery yeast bread is a German Christmas classic, studded with rum-spiked dried fruit and filled with homemade Marzipan.

Makes 2 loaves

1½ cups (192 grams) chopped dried apricots
1   cup (128 grams) dried cherries
½   cup (64 grams) golden raisins
½   cup (64 grams) raisins
½   cup (120 grams) dark rum
¾   cup (180 grams) warm water (105°F/41°C to 110°F/43°C)
4   tablespoons (48 grams) granulated sugar, divided
1   tablespoon plus 2 teaspoons (15 grams) active dry yeast
1   large egg (50 grams)
1   vanilla bean, split lengthwise, seeds scraped and reserved
1   orange (131 grams), zested
4   cups (500 grams) all-purpose flour
1   teaspoon (3 grams) kosher salt
½   teaspoon grated fresh nutmeg
½   teaspoon (1 gram) ground ginger
½   cup (113 grams) unsalted butter, softened
½   cup (57 grams) slivered almonds
¾   cup (195 grams) Marzipan (recipe follows)
2   tablespoons (28 grams) unsalted butter, melted
Confectioners' sugar, for sprinkling

1. In a medium bowl, toss together apricots, cherries, raisins, and rum. Cover and let stand for 12 hours.
2. In the bowl of a stand mixer fitted with the dough hook attachment, combine ¾ cup (180 grams) warm water, 1 tablespoon (12 grams) granulated sugar, and yeast. Let stand until mixture is foamy, about 10 minutes. With mixer on medium speed, add egg, vanilla bean seeds, zest, and remaining 3 tablespoons (36 grams) granulated sugar, beating until combined.
3. In a large bowl, whisk together flour, salt, nutmeg, and ginger. With mixer on low speed, gradually add flour mixture to sugar mixture, beating until combined. Add butter, 1 tablespoon (14 grams) at a time, beating until a smooth dough forms, 5 to 8 minutes.
4. Spray a large bowl with cooking spray. Place dough in bowl, turning to grease top. Cover and let rise in a warm, draft-free place (75°F/24°C) until doubled in size, 1 to 2 hours.
5. Line a baking sheet with parchment paper.

6. Turn out dough onto a lightly floured surface. Knead fruit mixture and almonds into dough, discarding any remaining liquid. Cover and let stand for 10 minutes. Divide dough in half. Pat one half of dough into an 8-inch square. Divide Marzipan in half, and shape each half into an 8x1-inch cylinder. Place one cylinder of Marzipan at one end of dough square, and roll up. Pinch ends under, and place on prepared pan. Repeat with remaining dough and remaining Marzipan. Cover and let rise in a warm, draft-free place (75°F/24°C) until puffed, 30 minutes to 1 hour.
7. Preheat oven to 350°F (180°C).
8. Bake until golden brown and an instant-read thermometer inserted in center registers 190°F (88°C), 35 to 40 minutes, covering with foil halfway through baking to prevent excess browning, if necessary. Brush loaves with melted butter, and sprinkle with confectioners' sugar. Wrap tightly in plastic wrap, and store at room temperature for up to 2 weeks.

MARZIPAN
Makes about 1 cup

2¼ cups (216 grams) almond flour
1½ cups (180 grams) confectioners' sugar
1   large egg white (30 grams)
2   teaspoons (10 grams) rose water
2   teaspoons (8 grams) almond extract

1. In the work bowl of a food processor, place almond flour and confectioners' sugar; pulse until combined. Add egg white, rose water, and almond extract; process until mixture holds together. If mixture is too dry, add a bit of water, 1 teaspoon (5 grams) at a time. Wrap tightly in plastic wrap, and refrigerate for up to 1 month.

PANETTONE

Sweet and bready with a hint of rum, this mile-high Italian take on fruitcake may just become your new favorite. For perfect browning, be sure to use a panettone mold for baking—they're available at most specialty food stores.

Makes 1 (6-inch) panettone

1½	cups (192 grams) chopped dried apricots
½	cup (64 grams) dried cranberries
½	cup (64 grams) raisins
¼	cup (60 grams) dark rum
¼	cup (60 grams) hot water
⅔	cup (160 grams) warm water (105°F/41°C to 110°F/43°C)
⅔	cup (133 grams) granulated sugar, divided
1	teaspoon (3 grams) active dry yeast
5¾	cups (719 grams) all-purpose flour
1	tablespoon (21 grams) honey
3	large eggs (150 grams)
1	teaspoon (6 grams) vanilla bean paste
2	tablespoons (6 grams) orange zest
1	teaspoon (3 grams) kosher salt
10	tablespoons (140 grams) unsalted butter, softened
1	tablespoon (14 grams) cold unsalted butter

1. In a medium bowl, combine apricots, cranberries, raisins, rum, and ¼ cup (60 grams) hot water. Cover and let stand for at least 8 hours or overnight.

2. In the bowl of a stand mixer fitted with the paddle attachment, combine ⅔ cup (160 grams) warm water, 1 tablespoon (12 grams) sugar, and yeast. Let stand until mixture is foamy, about 10 minutes.

3. With mixer on medium-low speed, add flour, honey, eggs, vanilla bean paste, zest, salt, and remaining sugar, beating until combined. Add softened butter, 1 tablespoon (14 grams) at a time, letting each piece incorporate before adding the next. Increase mixer speed to medium-high, and beat until a smooth and elastic dough forms, about 8 minutes.

4. Drain fruit, discarding liquid. Reduce mixer speed to low. Add fruit, beating just until combined.

5. Spray a large bowl with cooking spray. Place dough in bowl, turning to grease top. Cover and let rise in a warm, draft-free place (75°F/24°C) until puffed, about 2 hours.

6. Transfer dough to refrigerator, and refrigerate for 12 to 15 hours.

7. Turn out dough onto a lightly floured surface. Shape into a ball by folding corners of dough into center. Butter and flour a 6-inch panettone mold. Place dough, seam side down, in prepared mold. Cover and let rise in a warm, draft-free place (75°F/24°C) until dough nearly reaches top of mold, 4 to 8 hours.

8. Preheat oven to 350°F (180°C).

9. Place panettone on a baking sheet. Using a sharp knife or lame, make a large "X" across top of loaf. Place cold butter in center of loaf.

10. Bake until an instant-read thermometer inserted in center registers 190°F (88°C), 1 to 1½ hours, covering with foil halfway through baking to prevent excess browning, if necessary. Remove from oven, and insert 2 long wooden or metal skewers into base of loaf (about 2 inches from bottom). Hang bread, upside down, from a deep stockpot to let cool completely, 30 minutes to 1 hour. (This prevents it from sinking.)

pull-apart
BREADS

THESE SWEET AND SAVORY
RECIPES ARE FOR BAKERS
WHO LOVE A HANDS-ON
EATING EXPERIENCE

HERB AND CHEESE MONKEY BREAD

The term "monkey bread" was first used in Southern California in the 1940s. Most commonly known as "pull-apart bread," it refers to a rich bread formed into separate pieces of yeast dough. This version is a savory twist on the classically sweet crowd-pleaser with four different flavors all baked into the same loaf. Your crew can pick around to eat their favorite or mix and match bites of all of them.

Makes 1 (10-inch) wreath

2   cups (480 grams) warm water (105°F/41°C to 110°F/43°C)
¼   cup (50 grams) granulated sugar
4½ teaspoons (14 grams) active dry yeast
5   cups (625 grams) all-purpose flour
1   tablespoon (9 grams) kosher salt
1   cup (227 grams) unsalted butter, melted and divided
½   cup (24 grams) chopped green onion
¼   cup (8 grams) chopped fresh parsley
3   tablespoons (6 grams) chopped fresh dill
⅓   cup (75 grams) whipped cream cheese
1   cup (100 grams) freshly grated Parmesan cheese
1   teaspoon (3 grams) garlic salt
¼   teaspoon garlic powder
1   cup (100 grams) shredded sharp Cheddar cheese
⅓   cup (47 grams) sesame seeds
¼   cup (36 grams) poppy seeds

1. In a medium bowl, combine 2 cups (480 grams) warm water, sugar, and yeast. Let stand until mixture is foamy, about 10 minutes.

2. In the bowl of a stand mixer fitted with the paddle attachment, stir together flour and salt. With mixer on low speed, add yeast mixture and ¼ cup (57 grams) melted butter, beating just until combined. Switch to the dough hook attachment. Beat at medium speed until dough is smooth and elastic, about 4 minutes.

3. Spray a large bowl with cooking spray. Place dough in bowl, turning to grease top. Loosely cover and let rise in a warm, draft-free place (75°F/24°C) until doubled in size, about 1 hour.

4. On a lightly floured surface, turn out dough. Punch dough down, and gently shape into a ball. Cover and let rest for 10 minutes. Using kitchen shears, snip dough into 1-inch (25-gram) pieces. Shape into 48 dough balls.

5. Preheat oven to 325°F (170°C). Butter and flour a 15-cup tube pan.

6. In a medium bowl, combine green onion, parsley, and dill. With your thumb, create a hole in the center of 12 pieces of dough. Spoon a heaping teaspoon of cream cheese into each hole, pressing dough edges together to seal. Dip filled dough balls in ½ cup (113 grams) melted butter, and roll in herb mixture.

7. In a small bowl, combine Parmesan, garlic salt, and garlic powder. Dip another 12 dough balls in same melted butter, and roll in Parmesan mixture.

8. In another small bowl, combine Cheddar and sesame seeds. Dip another 12 dough balls in melted butter, and roll in Cheddar mixture.

9. Dip remaining 12 dough balls in melted butter, and roll in poppy seeds.

10. Place dough balls in prepared pan, alternating flavor types, and pour remaining ¼ cup (57 grams) melted butter over dough.

11. Bake until an instant-read thermometer inserted near center registers 190°F (88°C), 50 to 55 minutes, loosely covering with foil halfway through baking to prevent excess browning, if necessary. Let cool in pan for 30 minutes. Remove from pan, and serve warm.

PESTO SUN-DRIED TOMATO ROLLS

It's like pizza—but so much prettier. This basil-tomato bread feeds our Italian cravings and is the perfect appetizer for summer gatherings. We promise you won't have leftovers.

Makes 14

Basic Pull-Apart Bread Dough (recipe follows)
Pesto (recipe follows)
1 (8-ounce) jar (227 grams) oil-packed
   sun-dried tomatoes, drained and roughly chopped
6 ounces (175 grams) goat cheese, crumbled

1. Butter and flour a 10-inch round cake pan.
2. On a lightly floured surface, turn out Basic Pull-Apart Bread Dough. Punch dough down, and gently shape into a ball. Cover and let rest for 10 minutes.
3. Roll dough into a 16x14-inch rectangle. Spread Pesto onto dough, and sprinkle with sun-dried tomatoes and goat cheese. Starting with one long side, roll up dough, jelly roll style, and press edge to seal. Slice into 14 rolls. Place rolls in prepared pan. Cover and let rise in a warm, draft-free place (75°F/24°C) until doubled in size, about 45 minutes.
4. Preheat oven to 350°F (180°C).
5. Bake until golden brown, about 30 minutes. Let cool in pan for 30 minutes.

BASIC PULL-APART BREAD DOUGH

Makes 14 rolls

⅔ cup (160 grams) warm whole milk (105°F/41°C to 110°F/43°C)
1 tablespoon (12 grams) granulated sugar
2¼ teaspoons (7 grams) active dry yeast
3¼ cups (406 grams) all-purpose flour, divided
¼ cup (57 grams) unsalted butter, melted
2 large eggs (100 grams)
1 teaspoon (3 grams) kosher salt

1. In the bowl of a stand mixer fitted with the paddle attachment, combine warm milk, sugar, and yeast. Let stand until mixture is foamy, about 10 minutes.

2. With mixer on low speed, add 1 cup (125 grams) flour, beating just until combined. Add melted butter and ½ cup (63 grams) flour, beating until combined. Beat in eggs. Gradually add salt and remaining 1¾ cups (218 grams) flour, beating until a soft dough forms. (Dough will be sticky.)
3. Spray a large bowl with cooking spray. Place dough in bowl, turning to grease top. Loosely cover and let rise in a warm, draft-free place (75°F/24°C) until doubled in size, about 1 hour.

PESTO

Makes ½ cup

2 cups (45 grams) fresh basil
1 cup (142 grams) walnuts
¾ cup (75 grams) freshly grated Parmesan cheese
3 cloves garlic (15 grams)
1 tablespoon (15 grams) fresh lemon juice
⅓ cup (75 grams) olive oil
Salt and pepper, to taste

1. In the work bowl of a food processor, pulse together basil, walnuts, Parmesan, garlic, and lemon juice until finely chopped and well combined. With processor running, add oil in a slow, steady stream until incorporated. Add salt and pepper to taste. Refrigerate in an airtight container for up to 1 week, or freeze for up to 2 months.

MAPLE BACON CHEDDAR PICKLE LOAF

Pickles? In bread? Oh, heck yes. The brininess of the pickles is what makes this savory bread so brilliant.

Makes 1 (9x5-inch) loaf

8   slices thick-cut bacon (230 grams)
¼   cup (85 grams) pure maple syrup
Basic Pull-Apart Bread Dough (recipe follows)
4   tablespoons (56 grams) unsalted butter, melted and divided
1   (8-ounce) block (225 grams) sharp Cheddar cheese, shredded
1   cup (186 grams) bread-and-butter pickles, chopped

1. Preheat oven to 350°F (180°C). Line a baking sheet with foil and parchment paper.
2. Place bacon slices on prepared pan. Drizzle maple syrup over bacon. Bake until crisp, 25 to 30 minutes. Let cool on a wire rack; crumble bacon.
3. On a lightly floured surface, turn out Basic Pull-Apart Bread Dough. Punch dough down, and gently shape into a ball. Cover and let rest for 10 minutes.
4. Roll dough into an 18x16-inch rectangle. Brush with 2 tablespoons (28 grams) melted butter, and sprinkle with bacon, Cheddar, and pickles. Using a knife or pizza wheel, slice dough lengthwise into 4 equal strips. Stack strips one on top of the other, and cut into 4x3-inch rectangles.
5. Spray a 9x5-inch loaf pan with cooking spray, and prop pan at an angle on a book or other object so pan is not flat.
6. Stack rectangles on their sides in prepared pan. Top with any fillings that came loose. Loosely cover and let rise in a warm, draft-free place (75°F/24°C) until doubled in size, 30 minutes to 1 hour.
7. Preheat oven to 350°F (180°C).
8. Drizzle remaining 2 tablespoons (28 grams) melted butter on top of loaf.
9. Bake until golden brown, 40 to 45 minutes, covering with foil halfway through baking to prevent excess browning, if necessary. Let cool in pan for 20 minutes before inverting onto a serving plate. Turn right-side up to serve.

BASIC PULL-APART BREAD DOUGH

Makes 1 (9x5-inch) loaf

⅔   cup (160 grams) warm whole milk (105°F/41°C to 110°F/43°C)
1   tablespoon (12 grams) granulated sugar
2¼   teaspoons (7 grams) active dry yeast
3¼   cups (406 grams) all-purpose flour, divided
¼   cup (57 grams) unsalted butter, melted
2   large eggs (100 grams)
1   teaspoon (3 grams) kosher salt

1. In the bowl of a stand mixer fitted with the paddle attachment, combine warm milk, sugar, and yeast. Let stand until mixture is foamy, about 10 minutes.
2. With mixer on low speed, add 1 cup (125 grams) flour, beating just until combined. Add melted butter and ½ cup (63 grams) flour, beating until combined. Beat in eggs. Gradually add salt and remaining 1¾ cups (218 grams) flour, beating until a soft dough forms. (Dough will be sticky.)
3. Spray a large bowl with cooking spray. Place dough in bowl, turning to grease top. Loosely cover and let rise in a warm, draft-free place (75°F/24°C) until doubled in size, about 1 hour.

BANANAS FOSTER MONKEY BREADS

Everyone loves monkey bread. Everyone also loves bananas Foster, a dessert created at New Orleans' Brennan's Restaurant in the early 1950s. We simply put two and two together. The result? This magic mess.

Makes 9

¼ cup (57 grams) unsalted butter
1 cup (220 grams) firmly packed light brown sugar
½ cup (120 grams) heavy whipping cream, warmed
2 tablespoons (30 grams) bourbon
⅛ teaspoon kosher salt
4 ripe bananas (496 grams), sliced
Basic Pull-Apart Bread Dough (recipe follows)
¾ cup (150 grams) granulated sugar
1½ teaspoons (3 grams) ground cinnamon

1. Spray 9 wells of 2 (6-cup) jumbo muffin pans with cooking spray.
2. In a large skillet, melt butter over medium-high heat. Add brown sugar; cook, stirring occasionally, until mixture is amber colored, 3 to 4 minutes. Remove from heat, and stir in warm cream, bourbon, and salt. Add sliced bananas, tossing to coat. Set aside until slightly thickened and cool enough to handle, 15 to 20 minutes.
3. On a lightly floured surface, turn out Basic Pull-Apart Bread Dough. Punch dough down, and gently shape into a ball. Cover and let rest for 10 minutes.
4. In a medium bowl, stir together granulated sugar and cinnamon.
5. Using kitchen shears, snip dough into ½-inch pieces. Roll dough pieces in cooled caramel sauce, and dredge in sugar mixture to coat. Place about 1 tablespoon caramel and bananas in bottom of each prepared muffin cup. Top with 3 to 4 sugar-coated dough balls. Repeat layers, drizzling with caramel and bananas, and topping with 3 to 4 more dough balls. Drizzle once more with caramel and bananas. Place muffin pans in a roasting pan (to prevent dripping into bottom of oven). Let rise in a warm, draft-free place (75°F/24°C) for 25 to 30 minutes.
6. Preheat oven to 350°F (180°C).
7. Bake until golden brown, 30 to 35 minutes. Let cool in pan for 10 minutes. Turn monkey breads out onto their tops to let cool completely. (This will allow the caramel to harden slightly so they can be served right-side up without completely falling apart.) Serve warm with a drizzle of any remaining caramel.

BASIC PULL-APART BREAD DOUGH
Makes 9 monkey breads

⅔ cup (160 grams) warm whole milk (105°F/41°C to 110°F/43°C)
1 tablespoon (12 grams) granulated sugar
2¼ teaspoons (7 grams) active dry yeast
3¼ cups (406 grams) all-purpose flour, divided
¼ cup (57 grams) unsalted butter, melted
2 large eggs (100 grams)
1 teaspoon (3 grams) kosher salt

1. In the bowl of a stand mixer fitted with the paddle attachment, combine warm milk, sugar, and yeast. Let stand until mixture is foamy, about 10 minutes.
2. With mixer on low speed, add 1 cup (125 grams) flour, beating just until combined. Add melted butter and ½ cup (63 grams) flour, beating until combined. Beat in eggs. Gradually add salt and remaining 1¾ cups (218 grams) flour, beating until a soft dough forms. (Dough will be sticky.)
3. Spray a large bowl with cooking spray. Place dough in bowl, turning to grease top. Loosely cover and let rise in a warm, draft-free place (75°F/24°C) until doubled in size, about 1 hour.

SWEDISH SAFFRANSKRANS

While baking, our orange-and-cardamom marmalade filling oozes out of the dough to caramelize on the crust. Swedish pearl sugar and almond slices deliver the perfect crunch. We suggest sprinkling on more of both before serving for added texture.

Makes 1 (12-inch) wreath

1	teaspoon saffron threads
½	teaspoon (1.5 grams) kosher salt
1	tablespoon (15 grams) vodka
1¼	cups (300 grams) warm whole milk (115°F/46°C to 120°F/49°C)
2	large eggs (100 grams), divided
4	cups (508 grams) bread flour
½	cup (100 grams) granulated sugar
1	tablespoon (6 grams) instant yeast
⅓	cup (76 grams) unsalted butter, softened and cubed
	Orange Marmalade Filling (recipe follows)
½	cup (64 grams) golden raisins
½	cup (85 grams) diced Candied Orange Peel (recipe follows)
1	teaspoon (5 grams) water
1	tablespoon (7 grams) sliced almonds
2	teaspoons (8 grams) Swedish pearl sugar

1. In a mortar, grind saffron threads and salt with a pestle. Add vodka, and let stand for 30 minutes.

2. In a small bowl, whisk together warm milk, 1 egg (50 grams), and saffron mixture. In the bowl of a stand mixer fitted with the dough hook attachment, stir together flour, granulated sugar, and yeast. With mixer on low speed, gradually add milk mixture, beating until just combined. Increase mixer speed to medium-low, and beat until well combined. Add butter, a few pieces at a time, beating until combined. Increase mixer speed to medium, and beat until smooth and elastic, about 7 minutes.

3. Spray a large bowl with cooking spray. Place dough in bowl, turning to grease top. Cover directly with plastic wrap, and let rise in a warm, draft-free place (75°F/24°C) until doubled in size, about 1 hour.

4. Line a large baking sheet with parchment paper.

5. On a lightly floured surface, roll dough into an 18x12-inch rectangle. Spread Orange Marmalade Filling onto dough, leaving a ½-inch border on all sides. Sprinkle with golden raisins and diced Candied Orange Peel. Starting at one long side, roll up dough, jelly

roll style; press edge to seal. Place on prepared pan. Form into a circle, pinching ends to seal.

6. Using kitchen scissors, make a 45-degree cut into dough, leaving about ¼ inch of dough uncut. (Be careful not to cut all the way through dough.) Make a second cut ½ inch from first cut. Repeat process around the circle until you reach first cut.

7. Using your hands, gently pull and lay alternating pieces in opposite directions, either pulling toward the center of the circle or pulling toward the outside of the circle. (Make sure not to tear pieces completely off.) Loosely cover with plastic wrap, and let stand in a warm, draft-free place (75°F/24°C) for 30 minutes.

8. Preheat oven to 350°F (180°C).

9. In a small bowl, whisk together 1 teaspoon (5 grams) water and remaining 1 egg (50 grams). Brush wreath with egg wash. Sprinkle with almonds and pearl sugar.

10. Bake until golden brown and an instant-read thermometer inserted in center registers 190°F (88°C), about 40 minutes, covering with foil to prevent excess browning, if necessary. Let cool completely on a wire rack. Store in an airtight container at room temperature for up to 4 days.

ORANGE MARMALADE FILLING
Makes about ½ cup

⅓	cup (107 grams) sweet orange marmalade
3	tablespoons (42 grams) unsalted butter, melted
1	teaspoon (2 grams) ground cardamom

1. In a small bowl, whisk together all ingredients until combined. Use immediately, or refrigerate for up to 5 days.

CANDIED ORANGE PEEL
Makes about 1 cup

1	large orange (131 grams)
1½	cups (360 grams) water
2	cups (400 grams) granulated sugar, divided

1. Peel orange, and slice peel into ¼-inch-thick strips.

2. In a small saucepan, bring peel and water to cover by 1 inch to a boil over medium heat. Cook for 15 minutes. Drain, and rinse with cold water.

3. In same pan, bring 1½ cups (360 grams) water and 1½ cups (300 grams) sugar to a boil over medium heat. Add peel. Reduce heat to medium-low, and simmer until peel is softened, 25 to 30 minutes. Drain.

4. Line a rimmed baking sheet with parchment paper.

5. Toss peel with remaining ½ cup (100 grams) sugar, and place on prepared pan. Let stand until dry, 1 to 2 days. Freeze in an airtight container for up to 2 months.

1. Starting at one long side, roll up dough, jelly roll style.

2. Make 45-degree cuts into dough, leaving about ¼ inch of dough uncut. Gently arrange alternating pieces toward or away from the wreath's center.

PARMESAN GOUDA FANTAILS

The nutty flavor of Gouda pairs well with the beer and yeast in this recipe, but you can easily swap Muenster, Edam, or Monterey Jack cheese in place of the Gouda, if desired.

Makes 12

1 cup (240 grams) room temperature Kölsch or Pilsner beer, divided
1 tablespoon (12 grams) granulated sugar
2¼ teaspoons (7 grams) active dry yeast
6 tablespoons (84 grams) unsalted butter, melted
3 cups (375 grams) all-purpose flour, divided
⅓ cup (33 grams) freshly grated Parmesan cheese
2 cloves garlic (10 grams), finely grated
4 tablespoons (8 grams) minced fresh parsley, divided
1 teaspoon (3 grams) kosher salt
6 ounces (175 grams) Gouda cheese, grated
2 tablespoons (28 grams) unsalted butter

1. In a medium microwave-safe bowl, microwave ¼ cup (60 grams) beer until it reaches 105°F(41°C) to 110°F(43°C), about 10 seconds. Add sugar and yeast, stirring to combine. Let stand until mixture is foamy, about 5 minutes. Stir in melted butter and remaining ¾ cup (180 grams) beer.

2. In the bowl of a stand mixer fitted with the paddle attachment, beat 2 cups (250 grams) flour, Parmesan, half of garlic, 3 tablespoons (6 grams) parsley, and salt at medium speed until combined. Add yeast mixture, beating to combine, about 1 minute. Gradually add remaining 1 cup (125 grams) flour, beating until dough begins to pull away from sides of bowl, about 3 minutes. Cover with plastic wrap, and let rise in a warm, draft-free place (75°F/24°C) for 45 minutes.

3. Spray a 12-cup muffin pan with cooking spray.

4. Punch down dough, and divide in half. Pat one half into a square. On a lightly floured surface, roll dough into a 12-inch square. Sprinkle with half of Gouda, and press into dough. Using a sharp knife, cut dough into 6 equal strips. Stack strips, cheese side up; cut crosswise into 6 equal pieces. Place each piece on its side in prepared muffin cups. Repeat with remaining dough and remaining Gouda.

5. Slightly separate layers of each roll. Cover loosely with plastic wrap, and let rise in a warm, draft-free place (75°F/24°C) until dough fills cups, 30 to 45 minutes.

6. Preheat oven to 375°F (190°C).

7. Bake until golden brown, 20 to 24 minutes.

8. In a small saucepan, melt butter over medium heat. Add remaining garlic and remaining 1 tablespoon (2 grams) parsley; cook until fragrant. Brush warm fantails with butter mixture. Let cool for at least 10 minutes before serving.

Recipe by Marian Cooper Cairns / Photo by Matt Armendariz

BRIOCHE À TÊTE

The French name of this brioche refers to the shape (tête means "head"). One of the most recognizable forms of brioche, it's noted by a smaller dome (the head) atop the larger round loaf. It's often simply called a Parisienne.

Makes 1 (8-inch) round loaf

Basic Brioche Dough (recipe follows)
1   large egg (50 grams), lightly beaten

1. Butter and flour a large brioche à tête mold.
2. Portion Basic Brioche Dough into 6 (160- to 165-gram) balls. Arrange balls in prepared mold. Cover and let rise in a warm, draft-free place (75°F/24°C) until dough is puffed, 1 to 1½ hours.
3. Preheat oven to 400°F (200°C).
4. Brush top of loaf with egg wash.
5. Bake for 15 minutes. Reduce oven temperature to 350°F (180°C), and bake until golden brown and an instant-read thermometer inserted in center registers 190°F (88°C), 35 to 40 minutes more.

BASIC BRIOCHE DOUGH
Makes 1 large Brioche à Tête

⅓   cup (80 grams) warm whole milk (80°F/27°C to 100°F/38°C)
3   tablespoons (36 grams) granulated sugar
1   tablespoon (9 grams) active dry yeast
3¼   cups (406 grams) all-purpose flour, divided
5   large eggs (250 grams), room temperature
1   teaspoon (3 grams) kosher salt
1   cup (227 grams) unsalted butter, softened

1. In the bowl of a stand mixer fitted with the paddle attachment, combine warm milk, sugar, and yeast. Let stand until mixture is foamy, about 10 minutes.

2. With mixer on medium-low speed, add 1½ cups (188 grams) flour and eggs, beating until smooth, 2 to 3 minutes. Cover and let stand for 30 to 45 minutes.
3. Switch to the dough hook attachment. Add salt and remaining 1¾ cups (218 grams) flour; beat at medium speed until a smooth and elastic dough forms and pulls away from sides of bowl, 8 to 10 minutes.
4. With mixer on medium speed, add butter, 1 tablespoon (14 grams) at a time, letting each piece incorporate before adding the next.
5. Spray a large bowl with cooking spray. Place dough in bowl, turning to grease top. Cover and let rise in a warm, draft-free place (75°F/24°C) until doubled in size, 1½ to 2½ hours.
6. On a lightly floured surface, turn out dough, and fold a few times to knock out a bit of air. Return dough to greased bowl; cover and refrigerate for at least 8 hours or overnight.

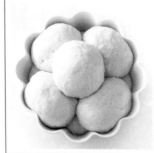

PRO TIP
To get the right shape, you'll need a specific brioche à tête pan, a fluted loaf pan that's easily found at stores such as Food52, Sur La Table, Williams Sonoma, and World Market.

BLACKBERRY JAM STAR

This jammy pull-apart is a brunchtime showstopper.

Makes 1 (9-inch) round star

Basic Pull-Apart Bread Dough (recipe on page 187)
4½ tablespoons (90 grams) blackberry jam or preserves, divided
1   large egg (50 grams), lightly beaten

1. On a lightly floured surface, turn out Basic Pull-Apart Bread Dough. Punch dough down, and gently shape into a ball. Cover and let rest for 10 minutes.
2. Divide dough into 4 equal pieces, and shape each piece into a ball. Roll first ball into a 9½-inch circle, and place on a sheet of parchment paper on a baking sheet. Press a 9-inch round cake pan over dough to make an indentation that will serve as your guide. Spread 1½ tablespoons (30 grams) jam onto dough, being careful to stay inside the impression you created with the pan.
3. Roll second ball of dough into a 9½-inch circle (it doesn't have to be perfect—the edges will be trimmed), and place on top of the first jam layer. Make another indentation with cake pan, and spread with 1½ tablespoons (30 grams) jam. Roll third ball into a 9½-inch circle, and spread with remaining 1½ tablespoons (30 grams) jam. Roll fourth ball into a 9½-inch circle, and place on top. Mark the edge with the cake pan, and trim around edges of all four layers with a sharp paring knife, discarding excess dough. Loosely cover with plastic wrap, and refrigerate until slightly firm, 20 to 30 minutes.
4. Mark the center of the circle, and make a 2½-inch-diameter indentation around it with a round cutter or measuring cup. Using a paring knife, make 12 or 16 cuts equidistant from the outer edge of the inner circle to the edge of the large circle, cutting through all four layers. Take two adjacent strips, and twist them away from each other twice. Use your finger to seal the inner seam. Turn the outer corners under, and press to seal. Repeat with all remaining strips. (See

technique photos on pages 198-199.) Loosely cover with plastic wrap, and refrigerate for at least 30 minutes or up to 2 hours.
5. Preheat oven to 350°F (180°C).
6. Brush dough with egg wash.
7. Bake until golden and puffed, 23 to 30 minutes. Serve warm.

BASIC PULL-APART BREAD DOUGH
Makes 9 monkey breads or 1 (9-inch) round star (recipe on page 197)

⅔   cup (160 grams) warm whole milk (105°F/41°C to 110°F/43°C)
1   tablespoon (12 grams) granulated sugar
2¼   teaspoons (7 grams) active dry yeast
3¼   cups (406 grams) all-purpose flour, divided
¼   cup (57 grams) unsalted butter, melted
2   large eggs (100 grams)
1   teaspoon (3 grams) kosher salt

1. In the bowl of a stand mixer fitted with the paddle attachment, combine warm milk, sugar, and yeast. Let stand until mixture is foamy, about 10 minutes.
2. With mixer on low speed, add 1 cup (125 grams) flour, beating just until combined. Add melted butter and ½ cup (63 grams) flour, beating until combined. Beat in eggs. Gradually add salt and remaining 1¾ cups (218 grams) flour, beating until a soft dough forms. (Dough will be sticky.)
3. Spray a large bowl with cooking spray. Place dough in bowl, turning to grease top. Loosely cover and let rise in a warm, draft-free place (75°F/24°C) until doubled in size, about 1 hour.

1 Divide dough into 4 equal pieces, and shape into balls. On a sheet of parchment paper, roll one piece of dough into a 9½-inch circle.

2 Use a 9-inch cake pan to make an indentation in the dough.

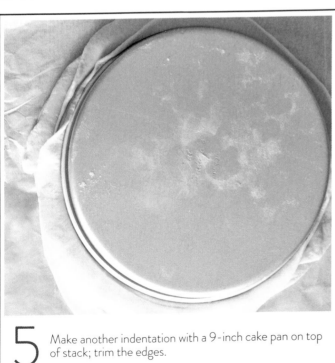

5 Make another indentation with a 9-inch cake pan on top of stack; trim the edges.

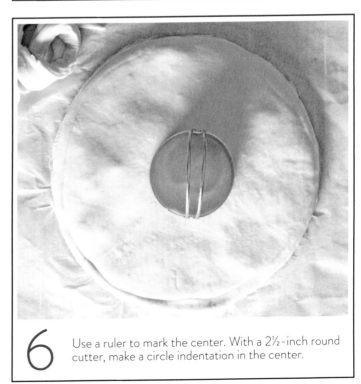

6 Use a ruler to mark the center. With a 2½-inch round cutter, make a circle indentation in the center.

BLACKBERRY JAM STAR
HOW-TO

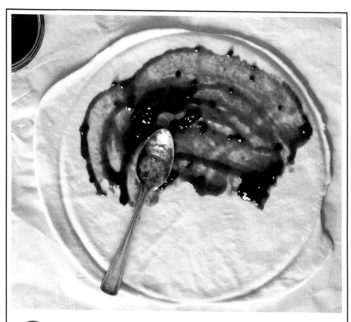

3 Spread 1½ tablespoons (30 grams) jam onto dough round, being careful to stay inside the circle indentation.

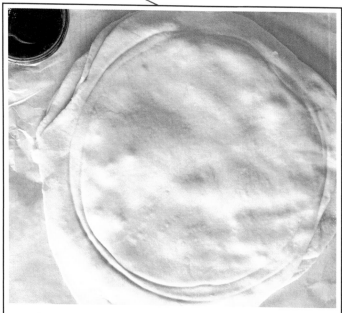

4 Roll out remaining pieces of dough into circles, and place atop first round, alternating dough and jam, finishing with the fourth and final circle of dough on top.

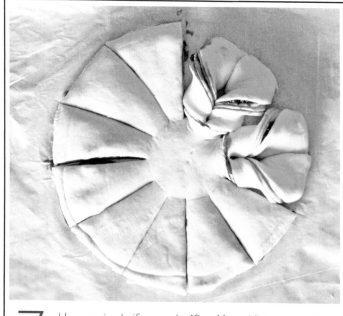

7 Use a paring knife to make 12 or 16 equidistant cuts all the way through the dough-jam stack, from the outside of the inner circle all the way to the outer edge.

8 Take two adjacent strips and twist them twice, away from each other, using your fingers to seal the inner seam. Repeat all the way around the loaf.

recipe index

credits

Front and Back Cover Photography by
Stephen DeVries

Photography by
Matt Armendariz, Stephen DeVries, Mason + Dixon

Recipe Development and Food Styling by
Marian Cooper Cairns, Ben Mims, Emily Turner

Styling by
Mason + Dixon